Grenada, St Vincent & the Grenadines

Sarah Cameron

Credits

Footprint credits

Editor: Stephanie Rebello
Production and layout: Emma Bryers
Maps: Kevin Feeney

Publisher: Patrick Dawson
Managing Editor: Felicity Laughton
Advertising: Elizabeth Taylor
Sales and marketing: Kirsty Holmes

Photography credits
Front cover: PHB.cz (Richard Semik)/
Shutterstock.com
Back cover: Laszlo Halasi/
Shutterstock.com

Printed in India by Thomson Press Ltd,
Faridabad, Haryana

Every effort has been made to ensure
that the facts in this guidebook are
accurate. However, travellers should
still obtain advice from consulates,
airlines, etc, about travel and visa
requirements before travelling. The
authors and publishers cannot accept
responsibility for any loss, injury or
inconvenience however caused.

The content of Footprint *Focus Grenada,
St Vincent and the Grenadines* is based
on Footprint's *Caribbean Islands
Handbook*, which was researched
and written by Sarah Cameron.

Publishing information

Footprint *Focus Grenada, St Vincent
and the Grenadines*
1st edition
© Footprint Handbooks Ltd
October 2014

ISBN: 978 1 909268 36 4
CIP DATA: A catalogue record for
this book is available from the
British Library

® Footprint Handbooks and the
Footprint mark are a registered
trademark of Footprint Handbooks Ltd

Published by Footprint
6 Riverside Court
Lower Bristol Road
Bath BA2 3DZ, UK
T +44 (0)1225 469141
F +44 (0)1225 469461
footprinttravelguides.com

Distributed in the USA by
National Book Network, Inc.

Contents

St Vincent Passage

La Soufrière ▲
Richmond○
Georgetown●

Vermont Nature Trail
Barrouallie● **5**◆ **6**■ ST VINCENT
Montreal Gardens
Kingstown□✈

THE GRENADINES
Port Elizabeth○
Princess Margaret Beach **7**■ BEQUIA
Isle à Quatre○
Baliceaux○

Caribbean Sea

The Pillories○
Lovell Village○
MUSTIQUE
Petit Mustique○

Savan○

CANOUAN○
✈ Charlestown

MAYREAU○ **8**■
Tobago Cays

Tobago Basin

UNION ISLAND○ ○Clifton

PETITE MARTINIQUE○

Sandy Island○ **4**◆
CARRIACOU ○Hillsborough

Sauteurs○
2■ Belmont Estate
Gouyave○ ▲ Mt St Catherine
Grand Étang National Park ◆ **3**■ Grenville○ GRENADA

St George's○ ■ **1**
✈

N
10 km
10 miles

Grenada, St Vincent and the Grenadines are part of the Windward group of Caribbean islands, which also include Dominica, St Lucia, Guadeloupe and Martinique, which are Départements of France. All the islands were at one time colonized by the French and even those which eventually became British still retain French names for many of the towns and villages. French influences can be seen in some old colonial buildings, with gingerbread fretwork and jalousie shutters.

The islands are a series of green volcanic peaks jutting out of the sea and forming a barrier between the Atlantic Ocean and the Caribbean Sea. Sulphur fumaroles and hot springs can be found on the biggest islands where the volcanoes are dormant but not dead, and even under the sea. There are large areas of lush rainforest with national parks protecting places of biodiversity or natural beauty on land or underwater.

The islands are a haven for birds with many endemic species although several of the parrots are endangered, while the sea is teeming with fish and other marine life including whales and dolphins. Hikers and birdwatchers are spoilt for choice in the larger islands and yachtsmen are similarly blessed when navigating among the smaller Grenadines, one of the world's most popular sailing destinations. The beautiful beaches offer up plenty of water sports including excellent diving.

After either an action-packed or relaxing day doing nothing on the beach, the rum flows. Sunset cocktails are followed by delicious local cuisine featuring freshly caught seafood and delicious tropical fruits and vegetables, enhanced by home grown organic cocoa, nutmeg, cinnamon and other spices.

Planning your trip

Best time to visit Grenada, St Vincent and the Grenadines

The climate is tropical. Grenada, St Vincent and the Grenadines are volcanic, mountainous and forested islands, attracting more rain than some other, more low-lying islands in the Caribbean. The driest and coolest time of year is usually December-April, coinciding with the winter peak in tourism as snow birds escape to the sun. However, there can be showers, which keep things green. Temperatures can fall to 20°C during the day, depending on altitude, but are normally in the high 20s, tempered by cooling trade winds. The mean annual temperature is about 26°C. At other times of the year the temperature rises only slightly, but greater humidity can make it feel hotter if you are away from the coast, where the northeast trade winds are a cooling influence. The main climate hazard is hurricane season, which runs from June to November. Tropical storms can cause flooding and mudslides. See also box, page 8.

Getting to Grenada, St Vincent and the Grenadines

Air

Grenada is well served with direct flights from Europe, North and South America as well as having good connections with other Caribbean islands for a two-centre holiday or some island-hopping by air. Airlines serving Grenada are **British Airways** (www.ba.com) and **Virgin Atlantic** (www.virgin-atlantic.com) from London Gatwick, Delta (www.delta.com) and **American Airlines** (www.aa.com) from New York JFK, **Conviasa** (www.conviasa.aero) from Isla Margarita with connections from Venezuela, **Caribbean Airlines** (www.caribbean-airlines.com) from New York, Orlando, Miami, Toronto and some Caribbean islands and **LIAT** (www.liatairline.com) from a range of Caribbean islands. Other airlines fly to Barbados from where there are connecting flights with LIAT, There are also some seasonal flights, such as **Condor** from Frankfurt and **Air Canada Vacations** from Toronto.

  Maurice Bishop International Airport (T473-4444555, www.mbiagrenada.com) is on Grenada, while the sister island of Carriacou has the smaller **Lauriston Airport** with a shuttle service between the two with SVG Air.

  St Vincent does not yet receive direct international long-haul flights to its **ET Joshua Airport** at Arnos Vale, but a new, larger airport, **Argyle International Airport**, is under construction, due to open 2014-2015. In the meantime, the main gateways are Barbados (where there is a St Vincent and the Grenadines

Don't miss...

Information Desk in the Arrivals Hall of Grantley Adams International Airport open from 1300 until the last plane leaves for St Vincent), Trinidad, Grenada, St Lucia, Martinique and Puerto Rico for connections from North America and Europe. There are small airports on Bequia, Mustique, Canouan and Union islands.

Sea
Unless you are on a yacht or a cruise ship it is not easy to get to Grenada or St Vincent by sea, although there is a ferry between Union Island (St Vincent) and Carriacou (Grenada), allowing island hopping throughout the Grenadines, see Transport, below.

Transport in Grenada, St Vincent and the Grenadines

Air
SVG Air (www.svgair.com), Grenadine Air Alliance (http://grenadine-air.com) and Mustique Airways (www.mustique.com) have daily flights between the islands of St Vincent, Bequia, Mustique, Canouan, Union Island, Carriacou and Grenada, with scheduled and charter flights to these and other neighbouring islands. They operate small aircraft with a maximum of 18 passengers and the weight of luggage allowed is determined by the weight of the passengers. You should expect to be weighed.

Road
Roads are in reasonable condition but look out for potholes and other weather damage and also for the deep storm drains at the edges of narrow roads as well

Hurricane season

June too soon July stand by August it must September remember October all over

In recent years there have been several late storms and the 'October all over' proved a myth. There was little hurricane activity in the region from the 1950s until the late 1980s. Many of the islands were not affected by hurricanes and residents thought little of them. Homes were not built to withstand severe storms. In 1989 this all started to change when several violent storms roared through the islands and Hurricane Hugo did untold damage in the US Virgin Islands. The next few years were relatively quiet but 1995 struck with a bang (three names were 'retired' in deference to the dead and injured) and was the start of a 10-year period that has gone down in history as the most active stretch on record for hurricanes. Analysts expect that this active hurricane era will last another two or three decades.

A hurricane develops in warm waters and air, which is why the tropics are known for hurricanes. Powered by heat from the sea they are steered by the easterly trade winds and the temperate westerly winds, as well as their own ferocious energy. In the Atlantic, these storms form off the African coast and move west, developing as they come into warmer water. Around the core, winds grow to great velocity, generating violent seas. The process by which a disturbance forms and strengthens into a hurricane depends on at least three conditions: warm water, moisture and wind pattern near the ocean surface that spirals air inward. Bands of thunderstorms form and allow the air to warm further and rise higher into the atmosphere. If the winds at these higher levels are light, the structure remains intact and allows for further strengthening. If the winds are strong, they will shear off the top and stop the development. If the system develops, a definite eye is formed around which the most violent activity takes place; this is known as the eyewall. The centre of the eye is relatively calm. When the eye passes over land those on the ground are often misled that the hurricane is over; some even abandon safe shelter, not aware that as the eye passes the other side of the eyewall will produce violent winds and the other half of the hurricane.

The word 'hurricane' is derived from the Amerindian 'Hurakan', both the Carib god of evil and also one of the Maya creator gods who blew his breath across the chaotic water and brought forth dry land. In the north Atlantic, Gulf of Mexico, Caribbean and the eastern Pacific they are called hurricanes, in Australia, cyclones or 'willy willy', and in the Philippines, 'baguio'. In the Western North Pacific tropical cyclones of hurricane force are called typhoons. The first time hurricanes were named was by an

Australian forecaster in the early 1900s who called them after political figures he disliked. During the Second World War US Army forecasters named storms after their girlfriends and wives. Between 1950-1952 they were given phonetic names (able, baker, charlie). In 1953 the Weather Bureau started giving them female names again. Today individual names (male and female) are chosen by the National Hurricane Center in Miami (www.nhc.noaa.gov) and submitted to the World Meteorology Organization in Geneva, Switzerland for approval. As a system develops, it is assigned a name in alphabetical order from the official list.

There is very good information before hurricanes hit any land, thanks to accurate weather data gathered by the Hurricane Hunters from Keesler Airforce Base in the USA. During the storm season they operate out of St Croix in the US Virgin Islands, where they are closer to storms. This elite group of men and women actually fly through the eye of a hurricane in C130 airplanes gathering critical information on the wind speeds and directions and other data. This is sent to the Miami Hurricane Center where a forecast is made and sent to all islands in the potential path so they can prepare for the storm. Most of the island governments are now well prepared to cope with hurricanes and have disaster relief teams in place, while many of the island resorts, especially the larger ones, have their own generators and water supplies.

While a hurricane can certainly pose a threat to life, in most cases if precautions are taken the risks are reduced. Some of the main hazards are storm surge, heavy winds and rains. There is usually disruption of services such as communications, internal transport and airline services. Ideally, if a hurricane is approaching, it is better for the tourist to evacuate the island. During the hurricane, which is usually 6-36 hours, you have to be shut up inside a closed area, often with little ventilation or light, which can be stressful. Some tourists think a hurricane will be 'fun' and want to remain on island to see the storm. This is not a good idea. If you do remain you should register with your local consulate or embassy and email to alert your family that communications may go down and that you will follow the rules of the emergency services. You should be prepared to be inconvenienced and to help out in the clearing up afterwards.

Local met office issues advisories:
Tropical storm watch be on alert for a storm which may pose threats to coastal areas within 36 hours.
Tropical storm warning the storm is expected within 24 hours.
Hurricane watch hurricane conditions could be coming in 36 hours.
Hurricane warning the hurricane is expected within 24 hours.

as speed bumps or dips. Grenada has a spectacular road along the Caribbean coast, but it is twisty and parts sometimes get washed away during heavy rains or high seas during hurricanes. The road running through the mountains across the middle of the island is also twisty but beautiful through the rainforest. Roads in the south around St George's out to the airport and the many marinas in the area are in good condition. St Vincent has few roads away from the centres of population in the south and it isn't even possible to drive all the way around the island, as they peter out in the north. Mudslides after heavy rain can cause disruption and it is best to ask for local advice. Roads are good around Kingstown and along the south coast to Arnos Vale and Villa. There are not many roads on the smaller islands of the Grenadines but they are generally paved.

Bus

Most, but not all, of the islands have a cheap bus service, which can be a minibus or, on Bequia, a pick-up truck with seats in the back. They stop on demand rather than at bus stops. Some will convert to a taxi to take you off route. They are a popular and colourful means of transport and give an opportunity to see local life and hear the music. On Grenada, look for the destination stickers in the windscreen to help you get the right minibus. They all have conductors who can help you get off at the right place if you ask. Fares range from EC$2.50-6.50, depending on distance. However, they are renowned for driving fast on the twisty roads, so if you are prone to car sickness this may not be for you. On Carriacou, minibuses run south from Hillsborough to Harvey Vale and north to Windward daily 0700-1200, 1300-1700, although they also run at night if there's a party going on. A bus on hire is a taxi. On St Vincent the 14-seater buses have names and are highly decorated. The main bus station is near the waterfront and market in Kingstown and all buses go from here to the east or west coasts from 0530 to 0100, Monday to Saturday, less frequently on Sundays.

Car

Drive on the left. Maps are often not accurate so navigation becomes particularly difficult on the larger islands. Car hire is readily available; the minimum age for hiring is usually 25 and most companies require a rental period of three days or more in July and August. On Grenada a local driver's permit costs EC$30/US$12 on production of your driver's licence from home. On St Vincent and the Grenadines, a local licence costs EC$65. There is car hire on St Vincent and Bequia but not on the smaller islands.

Cycling

Cycling on Grenada and St Vincent is a tough work-out, with steep hills and tight curves. It is also potentially dangerous, with pot holes and storm drains to avoid, traffic coming round a bend on the wrong side of the road and no

Hiking

Hiking is rewarding on all the islands, whether through the mountains and rainforest of Grenada and St Vincent accompanied by birdsong and forest sounds, or in the hills of the Grenadines with gorgeous views out to sea where yachts bob about between the scattered islands. There are guides and organized tours to take you hiking up La Soufrière on St Vincent, while on Grenada there are mountains, waterfalls and lakes to explore.

Hiking alone in remote areas is not recommended; start early to avoid the midday heat and always get back to base before sunset at 1800. Take waterproofs or wear clothing that will dry out quickly after a shower and carry plenty of water. A hat and sunscreen are also essential. Remember to walk on the right on roads so that you can see approaching vehicles. There is often nowhere to get off and oncoming traffic travels very fast. See also the box on page 48.

space to get off the road. However, the views are tremendous and there is good cycling both on- and off-road. On Grenada, the ride between Sauteurs and Victoria is peaceful with spectacular views. From Gouyave to St George's via Grand Étang is difficult but rewarding with some steep hills in the beautiful forest reserve and small, friendly communities. Allow five to six hours. Cycling is recommended on Carriacou and traffic is very light. However, there is potential for lots of flat tyres in the dry season as there is an abundance of cacti. Cycling is rewarding on St Vincent too. The ride between Layou and Richmond is a strenuous four hours one way, but absolutely spectacular. Expect long, steep hills and lots of them. Be careful in the north, which has a reputation as a drug-producing area. There is competitive road racing on both islands.

Ferry

Getting around by ferry is a tremendous experience, giving you a taste of life on the water but at a fraction of the price of chartering your own yacht. The small islands are highly dependent on sea transport and you will see a wide variety of goods and vessels being loaded and unloaded.

Grenada, Carriacou and Petite Martinique are linked by the hovercraft, the *Osprey*, which runs a daily 90-minute service between Grenada and Carriacou before going on to Petite Martinique. There are lovely views of the west coast of Grenada before you head out into open water with a good chance of seeing dolphins playing around the boat.

From Carriacou (Grenada) to Union Island (St Vincent) you have the choice of a small, 37-ft ferry, *MV Lady JJ*, or fishing boats of various sizes which operate a water taxi service. The ferry is the only vessel which charges a per person fare. Other boats charge for the hire of the boat and boat clearance fees, so can work out quite expensive if you are not in a group. *MV Lady JJ*, based in Ashton, Union Island does the 45-minute crossing to Hillsborough Monday and Thursday 0730, returning from Carriacou 1400, EC$35 one way, www.grenadinesconnection.com. Note that this is an international ferry and you must clear Customs and Immigration at the Police Station in Hillsborough at 1100 on the day of departure, or at the airport on Union the day before for the early crossing. On arrival at Ashton on Union you should go immediately to the airport at Clifton for Immigration formalities. The owner of *Lady JJ*, Troy Gellizeau, or his assistant (or the captain of any other boat you arrive on), will accompany you through all these formalities, which can take time, but probably no longer than similar procedures at an international airport, and the view is better.

From Union there are ferries calling at all the inhabited Grenadine Islands up to St Vincent. These range from the fast ferry, *MV Jaden Sun*, (http://jadeninc.com) which connects St Vincent with Bequia, Mustique, Canouan and Union Island, to the more leisurely mail boat, *MV Barracuda*, which has long been plying the waters from Kingstown, St Vincent, to Canouan, Mayreau and Union Island twice a week. Other ferries include the *Bequia Express* (www.bequiaexpress.com) and *MV Admiral II* (www.admiraltytransport.com) between Kingstown and Bequia, *MV Gemstar* and *MV Guidance* which sail from Kingstown to Canouan, Mayreau and Union Island, *MV Canouan Bay* to Canouan twice a week and the Mustique ferry, *MV Endeavour*, which runs four or five days a week to Mustique. Fares from St Vincent are around EC$25 to Mustique or Bequia, EC$50 to Canouan, EC$60 to Mayreau and EC$70 to Union. Always check schedules with the Tourist Office or your hotel, as the ferries are sometimes out of commission for essential repairs or are on a private charter. In the southern Grenadines, **Erika's Marine**, www.erikamarine.com, is always a useful source of information for boats around the islands.

Taxi

Taxis are plentiful and are available on land as well as water. On Grenada, taxis charge about EC$40/US$16 from the airport to Grand Anse hotels on arrival. For a list of fares from the airport see www.mbiagrenada.com. Trips anywhere usually cost about EC$4 per mile. Many companies offer tours as well as taxi service and the drivers are usually informative and fun. Water taxis scoot about between St George's and Grand Anse and also between Kingstown and Villa Beach, although they'll take you to other beaches if you prefer.

Price codes

Where to stay

$$$$ over US$150 $$$ US$66-150
$$ US$30-65 $ under US$30

Price codes refer to a standard double/twin room in high season.

Restaurants

$$$ over US$12 $$ US$7-12 $ under US$7

Price codes refer to the cost of a two-course meal, excluding drinks or service charge.

Where to stay in Grenada, St Vincent and the Grenadines

Grenada is particularly well served with good, mid-range, small hotels and guesthouses. Most of the hotels are in the southwest, close to the airport and the best beaches, but still small enough to be comfortable and friendly, catering for individual travellers, package tours and luxury getaways. The majority are in the Grand Anse area, although there are some delightful places to stay around the island in remote coves. In St George's there are more guesthouses than hotels. Hotel rooms are subject to a 10% service charge and 10% tax on accommodation, food and beverages. High season is mid-December to mid-April, July and August. There are often steep discounts in low season, when prices can be 30% lower, although on Carriacou hotels often shut during this period.

Homestays are another option. **Homestays Grenada**, www.homestays grenada.com, organize all sorts of accommodation, living with families around the island in their homes or in self-catering apartments or villas; many hosts are retired, returned from living abroad. Daily rates range from US$30 up to US$120 for a luxury apartment, including cleaning and linen change and may include breakfast and one other meal. Airport transfers and other services can be arranged.

Accommodation on **St Vincent and the Grenadines** ranges from the height of luxury on Mustique, or exclusivity on the private island of Petit St Vincent, to a simple guesthouse on St Vincent. Bequia is known for villa rentals, Canouan has a glitzy resort with championship golf course, while Union Island is low key and casual, frequented by the yachting fraternity. There are few large hotels, partly because of the lack of a large international airport to fly in tourists, although with the construction of the Argyle Airport this might change.

Food and drink in Grenada, St Vincent and the Grenadines

Food

As you might expect of islands, there is a wide variety of seafood on offer, which is fresh and tasty and served in a multitude of ways. Fish and seafood of all sorts are commonly available and are usually better quality than local meat. Beef and lamb are often imported from the USA or Argentina, but goat, pork and chicken are produced locally. There is no dairy industry to speak of, so cheeses are also usually imported. There is, however, a riot of tropical fruit and vegetables and a visit to a local market will give you the opportunity to see unusual and often unidentifiable objects as well as more familiar items found in supermarkets in Europe and North America but with 10 times the flavour.

The best bananas in the world are grown in the Windward Islands on small farms either organically or, at least, using the minimum of chemicals. They are cheap and incredibly sweet and unlike anything you can buy at home. You will come across many of the wonderful tropical fruits in the form of juices or ice cream. Don't miss the rich flavours of the soursop (chirimoya, guanábana), the guava, tamarind or the sapodilla (zapote). Breakfast buffets are usually groaning under the weight of tropical fruits, from the bananas, pineapples, melons, oranges and grapefruit to mango, of which there are dozens of varieties, papaya/pawpaw, carambola (star fruit) and sugar apple (custard apple or sweetsop). Mangoes in season drip off the trees and those that don't end up on your breakfast plate can be found squashed in abundance all over the roads. Caribbean oranges are often green when ripe, as there is no cold season to bring out the orange colour, and are meant for juicing not peeling. Portugals are like tangerines and easy to peel. Avocados are nearly always sold unripe, so wait several days before attempting to eat them. Avocado trees provide a surplus of fruit so you will be doing everyone a favour if you eat as many as possible.

Avocados have been around since the days of the Arawaks, who also cultivated cassava and cocoa, but many vegetables have their origins in the slave trade, brought over to provide a starchy diet for the slaves. The breadfruit, a common staple, rich in carbohydrates and vitamins A, B and C, was brought from the South Seas in 1793 by Captain Bligh, perhaps more famous for the mutiny on the *Bounty*. A large, round starchy fruit, usually eaten fried or boiled, it grows on huge trees with enormous leaves. Christophene is another local vegetable which can be prepared in many ways, but is delicious baked in a cheese sauce. Dasheen is a root vegetable with green leaves, rather like spinach, which are used to make the tasty and nutritious callaloo soup. Plantains are eaten boiled or fried as a savoury vegetable, while green bananas, known as figs, can be cooked before they are ripe enough to eat raw as a fruit.

The term 'provisions' on a menu refers to root or starchy vegetables: dasheen, yams, sweet potatoes, tannia, pumpkins, etc. The style of cooking is known as Creole and is a mixture of all the cultural influences of the islands' immigrants over the centuries, from starchy vegetables to sustain African slaves to gourmet sauces and garnishes dating from the days when the French governed the islands.

The movement of people along the chain of Caribbean islands means that you can also find rotis (pancake-like parcel of curried chicken and veg) from Trinidad and jerk meats from Jamaica, although these have been adapted from what you can expect on those islands. Fish and seafood are fresh and delicious, but make sure you only eat lobster and conch in season (September to April) to avoid overfishing.

The cooking on **Grenada** is generally very good. *Lambi* (conch) is very popular, as is *callaloo* soup (made with dasheen leaves), *souse* (a sauce made from pig's feet), pepper pot and pumpkin pie. The national dish is 'oildown', a stew of salt meat, breadfruit, onion, carrot, celery, dasheen and dumplings, cooked slowly in coconut milk. Wild meat (armadillo, iguana, manicou) can occasionally be found but should not be tried, as these animals are endangered. Of the many fruits and fruit dishes, try stewed golden apple or soursop ice cream. Nutmeg features in many local dishes, try nutmeg jelly for breakfast, ground nutmeg comes on top of rum punches. Nutmeg, cloves, allspice, cinnamon and other aromatic spices can all be found in the market in St George's, a feast for the senses and the reason why Grenada is called the 'spice island'. Cocoa is grown organically on the island and cocoa balls can be found in the market for cooking with or for making hot chocolate, but the real star is the local organic chocolate made by the **Grenada Chocolate Company**, www.grenadachocolate.com, so good that it is stocked by Waitrose in the UK.

On **St Vincent**, the breadfruit is intimately linked with the island's history and culture, as it was here that Captain Bligh brought the first breadfruit tree from Tahiti in 1793. A descendant of that tree grows in Kingstown's Botanical Gardens to this day. The design of a breadfruit tree leaf is commonly seen as an artistic decoration around the island and the national dish is roasted breadfruit and fried jack fish. Like Grenada, locally grown vegetables include yams, dasheen, eddoes, bananas, plantains, christophene, sweet potatoes and a variety of salads and peppers, from sweet to hot for seasoning. Locally caught fish varies according to the season, but you can find flying fish, tuna, bonito, mahi mahi and kingfish on the menu as well as lambi, lobster, squid and octopus. If you visit the village of Barrouallie, on the west coast, you can see them bringing in the local speciality of 'black fish', which is actually a short-finned pilot whale, which grows to about 18 ft. These pilot whales are classified as Lower Risk-Conservation Dependent on the IUCN Redlist. The village usually holds a fish festival on the first Friday of the month.

Drink

For non-alcoholic drinks, there is a range of refreshing fruit juices, including orange, mango, pineapple, grapefruit, lime, guava and passionfruit. Sorrel and mauby (made from a bark) are also very popular. Coconut water sold by vendors is always refreshingly cool and sterile. Coconuts are picked unripe when they are full of water. Other local soft drinks include tamarind, a bitter sweet drink made from the pods of the tamarind tree. Teas are made from a variety of herbs, often for medicinal purposes. Cocoa tea, however, is drunk at breakfast and is hot chocolate, usually flavoured with spices. Be sure to try the local sea-moss drink (a mixture of vanilla, algae and milk). Rum punches are excellent in Grenada. There are three makes of rum, whose superiority is disputed by the islanders, **Clark's Court**, **River Antoine** and **Westerhall Plantation Rum**, made by Westerhall Distilleries. All three can be visited for a tour and sampling of rum and products for sale. Several readers have endorsed **Westerhall Plantation Rum** for its distinct flavour and aroma. The term 'grog', for rum, is supposed to originate in Grenada: taking the first letters of 'Georgius Rex Old Grenada', which was stamped on the casks of rum sent back to England. Grenada Breweries brew **Carib Lager**, **Guinness** and non-alcoholic malt beers. The local beer on St Vincent is **Hairoun** and if you prefer something stronger, there is the **Sunset** rum.

Restaurants

Tax of 8% and service of 10% is usually added to the bill in Grenada, while 15% VAT and 10% service is added in St Vincent. If service is not included, 10-15% is expected. There is a wide range of places to eat on Grenada, from snack bars and fast food places to fine dining. Most of the restaurants are in St George's and the southern part of the island, catering to hotel guests, cruise ship passengers and yachties, as well as residents. Around the island there are plenty of roadside places for refreshment during a day tour and you won't go hungry. There are fewer restaurants on Carriacou, particularly at the upper end of the scale, but bars, cafés and family-run bistros serve good, filling and delicious meals. Kingstown has several restaurants in the centre serving local food or fast food, but the better restaurants are in the Villa beach area several miles east. At the bus station (Little Tokyo) you can buy freshly grilled chicken and corn cobs, good value and tasty. Cafés on the jetty by ferry boats serve excellent, cheap local food such as salt cod rolls with hot pepper sauce. There are snackettes and bars serving local specialities in villages around the island and on the Grenadines.

Festivals in Grenada, St Vincent and the Grenadines

Grenada

Late Jan Grenada Sailing Festival, www.grenadasailingfestival.com, is held over 4 days, based at Port Louis Marina, with international yacht racing, followed the next weekend by a Work Boat Regatta from Grand Anse beach. The latter attracts sailors from communities with a strong fishing or boat-building heritage, such as Grand Mal, Gouyave, Sauteurs, Woburn, Carriacou and Petite Martinique. Also at the end of Jan is the Budget Marine Spice Island Billfish Tournament, www.sibtgrenada.com, at Grenada Yacht Club.

7 Feb Independence Day. There is a military parade at Tanteen and lots of beach parties.

Mar/Apr Easter is a time for lots of events, both religious and otherwise. There is a **kite flying competition** at the old Pearls Airport, with music, food and drink, and other activities, and **yacht races** and a **power boat regatta** off Grand Anse.

Late Jun Throughout the island, but especially at Gouyave, the **Fisherman's Birthday** is celebrated (the feast of saints Peter and Paul); it involves the blessing of nets and boats, followed by dancing, feasting, street parties and boat races.

Early Aug Rainbow City Cultural Festival takes place in Grenville over the first weekend of Aug, with local arts and crafts, food, music and tours of the area. **Mid-Aug Spice Mas Festival**, www.spicemasgrenada.com, Grenada's **Carnival**, is held in the 2nd weekend of Aug (although some preliminary events and competitions are held from the last week in Jul), with calypsos, steel bands, dancing, competitions, shows and plenty of drinking. The Sun night celebrations, **Dimanche Gras**, continue into Mon, **J'Ouvert**; **Djab Djab Molassi**, who represent devils, smear themselves and anyone else (especially the smartly dressed) with black grease. On Mon a carnival pageant is held on the stage at Queen's Park and on Tue the bands parade through the streets of St George's to the Market Square and a giant party ensues. During Carnival it is difficult to find anywhere to stay and impossible to hire a car unless booked well in advance.

Nov Every month the **Grenada Yacht Club** (T4406826, www.grenadayachtclub.com) holds races off Grand Anse and there is usually an end-of-hurricane season yacht race at the end of Nov.

Carriacou

Feb Carriacou celebrates its **carnival** at the traditional Lenten time, unlike Grenada. It is not spectacular but it is fun and there is a good atmosphere, with parades, street dances and calypso competitions. An interesting feature is the **Shakespeare Mas**, when participants, or 'pierrots' (*paywos*) dress up and recite from Shakespeare's plays. If they forget their lines or get something wrong, they are thumped by the others with a bull whip, so their costumes require a lot of padding and they wear a special cape which covers the back of the head. It is very competitive and carnival has traditionally been very violent, with battles between villages or between north and south of the island, led by their carnival 'kings'. The police have in the past frequently had to restore peace.

End-Apr 3-day **Maroon and String Band Music Festival**, www.carriacoumaroon.com, a revival of traditional customs held in the historic Belair Park, Hillsborough and Paradise Beach. You can see a display of the **Big Drum Nation Dance**, string band music and quadrille dancing, as well as Shakespeare Mas and more modern entertainment, such as reggae. There are also stalls demostrating and selling local smoked food, cultural and art exhibitions.

Aug **Carriacou Regatta** on the 1st weekend, with races for work boats, yachts, model boats, donkeys and rowing boats, as well as the greasy pole, tug-o-war and cultural shows, see facebook.

Mid-Dec **Parang Festival**, http://carriacouparangfestival.com, runs over 3 evenings (Fri-Sun) the weekend before Christmas. It is a musical celebration: local groups perform Christmas carols on Fri at Silver Beach, Hillsborough. Sat is the most lively night with visiting Calypsonians and performers from Grenada and other islands at Belair Park judged by visiting dignitaries, and Sun is the competition between the Parang string bands.

Petite Martinique

May Petite Martinique holds a **Whitsuntide Regatta Festival**, www.petitemartinique.com/regatta, with lots of boat races and land-based fun and games such as the greasy pole, tug-of-war and even a crying competition.

St Vincent

Mar **National Heroes and Heritage Month**, with tributes and celebration of the national heroes, taking in National Heroes Day on 14 Mar, a public holiday.

Apr Fisherman's month.

Jun-Jul **St Vincent's Carnival**, called **Vincy Mas**, is held in the last week of Jun and the 1st week of Jul for 10 days. Mas is short for masquerade, and the 3 main elements of the carnival are the costume bands, the steel bands and the calypso. During the day there is **J'Ouverte, ole mas**, children's carnival and steel bands through Kingstown's streets. At night Calypsonians perform in 'tents', there is the **King and Queen** of the bands show, the steel bands competition and **Miss Carnival**, a beauty competition with contestants from other Caribbean countries (a talent contest, a beauty contest and local historical dress). Thousands of visitors come to take part, many from Trinidad.

Aug **Breadfruit Festival Month**.

Oct **Independence Celebrations**.

16-24 Dec **Carolling Competition and Nine Mornings Festival**, during which, for 9 mornings from 0400, people parade through Kingstown, enjoy sea baths, dances/fêtes, bike rides and street concerts. In rural areas the festival ends with a steel band jump-up. There is also an art and craft exhibition.

Grenadines

Jan Bequia holds a 4-day **Music Festival**, www.bequiatourism.com/bequiamusicfest, at the end of the month.

Jan/Feb Mustique Blues Festival, www.basilsbar.com, founded by Dana Gillespie and Basil Charles and held at and organized by Basil's Bar, features regional and international artistes.

Apr Easterval on Union Island, with music, dancing, beauty pageant and lots of entertainment. **Bequia Easter Regatta**, www.begos.com/easterregatta, organized by the Bequia Sailing Club at the Frangipani Hotel, with races in Friendship Bay and around the island.

May Mayreau holds its **Regatta** together with talent shows and after-race parties.

May/Jun Canouan Regatta is a big event on the island, with races, street parties, jump-ups, calypso competitions and beauty pageants.

Jul Canouan holds its **Carnival** at the end of the month.

Essentials A-Z

Accident and emergency

Grenada T911 for **Police** or **Fire**. The Police can also be called on T473-4391231 (rapid response) or T473-4444454, while the Fire service can be called on T473-4402112. T434 or T473-4402113 for **General Hospital Ambulance**, St George's, T724 in St Andrews or T774 on Carriacou. **St Vincent** T911 for **Police** or **Fire**, also T784-4571211 for the Police. **The Milton Cato Memorial Hospital** in Kingstown has A&E services, T784-4561185.

Clothing

Casual, lightweight summer clothes suitable all year. Bathing costumes are not accepted off the beach.

Currency

East Caribbean dollar, EC$.
US$1 = EC$2.67.

Electricity

220/240 volts, 50 cycles AC, except for Petit St Vincent which has 110 volts, 60 cycles. The British 3 rectangular pin plugs are used throughout the rest of the islands. However, most hotels provide dual voltage shaver units and many of the newer hotels have sockets for the US 2-pin plugs. Transformers/adaptors are usually available on request.

Embassies and consulates

For a full list of embassies and consulates in Grenada and St Vincent and the Grenadines and Grenadian and St Vincentian offices abroad, see http://embassy.goabroad.com/

Health

Travel in Grenada and St Vincent and the Grenadines poses no health risk to the average visitor provided sensible precautions are taken. It is important to see your GP or travel clinic at least 6 weeks before departure for general advice on any travel risks and necessary vaccinations. Try phoning a specialist travel clinic if your own doctor is unfamiliar with health conditions in the Windward Islands. Check with the National Health Service or health insurance on coverage in the islands and take a copy of your insurance policy with you. Also get a dental check, know your own blood group and, if you suffer a long-term condition such as diabetes or epilepsy, obtain a Medic Alert bracelet/necklace (www. medicalert.co.uk). If you wear glasses, take a copy of your prescription.

Vaccinations

It is important to confirm your primary courses and boosters are up to date. It is also advisable to vaccinate against tetanus, typhoid and hepatitis A. Vaccines sometimes advised are hepatitis B, rabies and diphtheria. Yellow fever vaccination is not required unless you are coming directly from an infected country in Africa or South America. Although cholera vaccination is largely ineffective, immigration officers may ask for proof of such vaccination if coming from a country where an epidemic has occurred. Check www.who.int for updates. Malaria is not a danger in Grenada or St Vincent and the Grenadines.

Health risks

The most common affliction of travellers to any country is probably **diarrhoea**. Tap water is good in most areas, but bottled water is widely available and recommended. Swimming in sea or river water that has been contaminated by sewage can be a cause of diarrhoea; ask locally if it is safe. Diarrhoea may also be caused by viruses, bacteria (such as E-coli), protozoal (such as giardia), salmonella and cholera. It may be accompanied by vomiting or by severe abdominal pain. Any kind of diarrhoea responds well to the replacement of water and salts. Sachets of rehydration salts can be bought in most pharmacies and can be dissolved in boiled water. If the symptoms persist, consult a doctor.

The major risks posed in the region are those caused by insect disease carriers such as mosquitoes and sandflies. The key parasitic and viral diseases are **dengue fever** and **chikungunya** (also known as chik V). Dengue fever and chikungunya are particularly hard to protect against as the mosquitoes can bite throughout the day as well as night (unlike those that carry malaria). Chikungunya virus is relatively new in the Caribbean. It does not kill, unlike dengue, but causes severed joint pain which can last for a year or 2 after infection. There is no malaria. There are lots of mosquitoes at certain times of the year, so take insect repellent and avoid being bitten as much as possible. Sleep off the ground and use a mosquito net and some kind of insecticide. Remember that DEET (Diethyltoluamide) is the gold standard. Apply the repellent every 4-6 hrs but more often if you are sweating heavily. If a non-DEET product is used, check who tested it. Validated products (tested at the London School of Hygiene and Tropical Medicine) include Mosiguard, Non-DEET Jungle formula and non-DEET Autan. If you want to use citronella remember that it must be applied very frequently (ie hourly) to be effective.

The climate is hot; the islands are tropical and protection against the sun will be needed. Do not be deceived by cooling sea breezes. To reduce the risk of **sunburn** and skin cancer, make sure you pack high-factor sun cream, light-coloured loose clothing and a hat.

If you get sick

There are public hospitals, medical centres and clinics, while the larger hotels have doctors on call. Make sure you have adequate insurance (see below). Remember you cannot dial any toll-free numbers abroad so make sure you have a contact number.

Useful websites

www.bgtha.org British Global and Travel Health Association.

www.cdc.gov Centers for Disease Control and Prevention; US government site that gives excellent advice on travel health and details of disease outbreaks.

www.fco.gov.uk British Foreign and Commonwealth Office travel site has useful information on each country, people, climate and a list of UK embassies/consulates.

www.fitfortravel.scot.nhs.uk A-Z of vaccine/health advice for each country.

www.sensitivescreening.com/mht. htm Number One Health Group offers travel screening services, vaccine and travel health advice, email/SMS text vaccine reminders and screens returned travellers for tropical diseases.

Insurance

All travellers should hold comprehensive travel insurance including medical insurance. Insurance should be valid for the full duration of your stay and should cover medical evacuation. You should check any exclusions, and that your policy covers you all for the activities you want to undertake, such as scuba diving or canyoning.

Language

English is the official language.

Money

The currency on both islands is the East Caribbean dollar, EC$, fixed at US$1 = EC$2.67.

Exchange

Banks will exchange major currencies, such as the US$, Can$, € and £. Some traders will accept US$, but you will get a better rate if you change your money at a bank. You will receive your change in EC$.

Plastic/currency cards/ATMs

Credit cards are accepted in the larger hotels, restaurants and shops, but cafés, rum shops and smaller operators only take cash. Banks nearly all have ATMs and accept all major international cards.

If you don't want to carry lots of cash, pre-paid currency cards allow you to preload money from your bank account, fixed at the day's exchange rate. They look like a credit or debit card and are issued by specialist money changing companies, such as **Travelex** and **Caxton FX**. You can top up and check your balance by phone, online and sometimes by text.

Cost of living/travelling

The islands are expensive, reflecting the need to import most daily essential items and the lack of any economies of scale. High season is Dec-Apr and Jul-Aug, when hotel prices are at their highest. Good deals can be found in hurricane season, particularly Sep-Nov. Cheap and cheerful lodging can be found for US$40-50 a night, but they will be inland, not on the beach. Generally, a room in a decent hotel or guesthouse will cost in the region of US$100 a night, or more for the luxury places. Some of the cheaper accommodation can only be reached with a rental car, unless you are in the city, which can be noisy, hot and uncomfortable. Renting a house or apartment is an option for a group so you can share the cost. Homestays are also good value. Eating in local cafeterias, drinking in rum shops and travelling on buses can save you money.

Official time

Atlantic Standard Time, 4 hrs behind GMT, 1 hr ahead of EST.

Opening hours

Grenada: **Banks**: Mon-Thu 0800-1300 or 1400; Fri 0800-1200 or 1300, 1430-1700. **Government offices**: Mon-Fri 0800-1145, 1300-1600. **Shops**: Mon-Fri 0800-1600, Sat 0800-1300, although tourist shops will be open if there is a cruise ship in port. **St Vincent**: **Banks**: Mon-Thu 0800-1500, Fri 0800-1700. **Government offices**: Mon-Fri 0800-1200, 1300-1615. **Shops**: Mon-Fri 0800-1600, Sat 0800-1200, although supermarkets open 0800-2000.

Public holidays

Grenada: New Year's Day (1 Jan), Independence Day (7 Feb), Good Fri and Easter Mon, Labour Day (1 May), Whit Monday (in May/Jun), Corpus Christi (Jun), Emancipation Day (1st Mon in Aug), Carnival Mon and Tue (2nd week in Aug), Thanksgiving (25 Oct), Christmas Day and Boxing Day (25 and 26 Dec).

St Vincent and the Grenadines: New Year's Day (1 Jan), National Heroes Day (14 Mar), Good Fri and Easter Mon, Labour Day in May, Whit Mon, Carnival Mon and Tue (in Jul), Emancipation Day (1st Mon in Aug), Independence Day (last Mon in Oct), Christmas Day (25 Dec) and Boxing Day (26 Dec).

Safety

The islands are relatively safe, but you still need to exercise caution, especially against petty theft or robbery, which should always be reported to the police. Do not leave your possessions unattended on the beach; leave valuables in the hotel safe and, if renting a car, keep everything out of sight and locked in the boot. Don't offer lifts to strangers. Street lighting is patchy so avoid dark streets at night. Do not go to out of the way or deserted beaches at night and do not sleep on the beach. There is smuggling and most crimes are related to drugs. In the port towns, hassling can be a nuisance on days when a cruise ship is in. The smaller islands are generally very safe, but if you are staying on a yacht you should make sure it is secure, day or night.

Tax

For stays of over 24 hrs on Grenada, departure tax is EC$50 (EC$25 for children 5-12), although this is often included in your plane ticket, so check. EC$10 airport tax is charged on departure from Lauriston Airport,

Carriacou, so if you are leaving that island with a flight connection in Grenada you will pay a total of EC$60. Departure tax from St Vincent and the Grenadines is EC$40.

Telephone

The international code for Grenada is 473 and St Vincent and the Grenadines is 784. Land line, mobile and roaming services are provided by **Lime**, www.lime.com, and **Digicel**, www.digicelgrenada.com or www.digicelsvg.com.

Tourist information

Tourism Authority, Box 293, Burn's Point, St George's, T473-4402279, www.grenadagrenadines.com. 0800-1600, very helpful, lots of leaflets. There is also a cruise ship office, T473-4402872, and tourist office at the airport, helpful, hotel reservation service, T473-4444140. On Carriacou, Main St, Hillsborough, beside the Osprey office, T473-4437948, carrgbt@spiceisle.com. The **Grenada Hotel and Tourism Association** is at Ocean House Building, Morne Rouge, T473-4441353, http://ghta.org. The **St Vincent and the Grenadines Tourism Authority** (SGVTA) is on the 2nd floor, NIS Building, Upper Bay St, Kingstown, T784-4566222, http://discoversvg.com, Mon-Fri 0800-1600. There are also information desks at **ET Joshua Airport**, Arnos Vale, T784-4584685, and at the cruise ship terminal, T784-4571592. The St **Vincent and the Grenadines Hotel and Tourism Association**, www.svghotels.com,

publishes *Ins and Outs of St Vincent and the Grenadines*, www.insandoutsofsvg.com. On the Grenadines, there are the **Bequia Tourism Association**, www.bequiatourism.com, **Friends of Union Island Tourism**, www.unionisland.com.

Visas and immigration

To enter Grenada or St Vincent and the Grenadines all visitors must have a passport (valid for 6 months after the date of entry) and an onward or return ticket. However, Grenada will allow entry by British, Canadian and US citizens with photo ID and proof of citizenship, although US citizens may not return to the USA without a passport under US restrictions. For visits to Grenada of up to 90 days, visas are not required for citizens of the USA, British Commonwealth, most European countries, Japan, South Korea and most of the Caribbean.

Visas for St Vincent and the Grenadines are required only from nationals of the Dominican Republic, Jordan, Syria, Lebanon, the People's Republic of China, Iraq, Iran and Nigeria. All visitors, except those from Caricom countries, will be granted a stay of 4 weeks, which you can extend on payment of EC$25. You will be asked where you will be staying on the island and will need a reservation, which can be done through the tourist office at the airport, before going through immigration.

Weights and measures

Imperial.

Contents

Footprint features

Grenada, St Vincent & the Grenadines

Grenada

Known as the spice island because of the nutmeg, mace and other spices it produces, Grenada (pronounced 'Grenayda'), the most southerly of the Windward Islands, has a beautiful mountainous interior and is well endowed with lush forests and cascading rivers. Hikers and nature lovers enjoy the trails of the national parks, where many different ecosystems are found, from dry tropical forest and mangroves on the coast, through lush rainforest on the hillsides, to elfin woodland on the peaks. St George's, the capital, is widely acknowledged as the prettiest harbour city in the West Indies, blending the architectural styles of the French and English with a picturesque setting on steep hills overlooking the bay. The southern coast, with its sandy beaches, bays and rocky promontories, is being developed for tourism. In 2004 Grenada was blown away by Hurricane Ivan, which killed dozens and destroyed or seriously damaged nearly every building on the island when the 'eye' of the storm passed directly over. Now, however, business is back to normal as Grenadians have bounced back, although some homes and churches have not yet been rebuilt.

Grenada

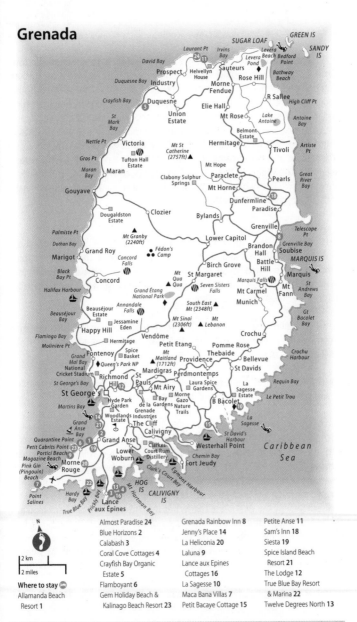

Where to stay 🛏

Allamanda Beach
Resort 1

Almost Paradise 24
Blue Horizons 2
Calabash 3
Coral Cove Cottages 4
Crayfish Bay Organic
  Estate 5
Flamboyant 6
Gem Holiday Beach &
  Kalinago Beach Resort 23

Grenada Rainbow Inn 8
Jenny's Place 14
La Heliconia 20
Laluna 9
Lance aux Epines
  Cottages 16
La Sagesse 10
Maca Bana Villas 7
Petit Bacaye Cottage 15

Petite Anse 11
Sam's Inn 18
Siesta 19
Spice Island Beach
  Resort 21
The Lodge 12
True Blue Bay Resort
  & Marina 22
Twelve Degrees North 13

St George's is one of the Caribbean's most beautiful harbour cities. The town stands on an almost landlocked sparkling blue harbour against a background of green and hazy blue hills, with its terraces of pale colour-washed houses and cheerful red roofs. The capital was established in 1705 by French settlers, and much of its charm comes from the blend of two colonial cultures: typical 18th-century French provincial houses intermingle with fine examples of English Georgian architecture. Unlike many Caribbean ports, which are built around bays on coastal plains, St George's straddles a promontory. It has steep hills with long flights of steps and sharp bends, with police on point duty to prevent chaos at the blind junctions. At every turn is a different view or angle of the town, the harbour or the coast.

Arriving in St George's

Getting there The airport is about five miles south of St George's at the southern tip of the island and there is a good road from there to the capital, which can be reached by car, taxi or bus. Cruise ships come in to a dedicated terminal on the waterfront while the ferry to and from Carriacou docks in the harbour and yachts use the lagoon.

Getting around The centre of St George's is small enough to walk around but it can be hot work negotiating the hills. Taxis and buses are plentiful if you prefer to get a ride.

Tourist information There is an information centre at the cruise ship terminal or you can go to the Tourism Authority head office at Burn's Point.

Places in St George's

The Carenage The Carenage runs around the inner harbour, connected with the Esplanade on the seaward side of Fort George Point by the **Sendall Tunnel**, built in 1895. There is always plenty of dockside activity on the Carenage, with goods being unloaded from wooden schooners. Cruise ships now come in to a new deep water cruise ship port on the Esplanade on the western side of the city, while the ferries and hovercraft from Carriacou and Petite Martinique still dock in the middle of the Carenage. Restaurants, bars and shops line the Carenage. The harbour is the crater of an old volcano. In 1867 the water in the lagoon started to boil and the air stank of sulphur. The water level in the harbour has risen about 5 ft above sea level on three occasions, causing flood damage on the Carenage.

The small **National Museum** ⓘ *corner of Young and Monckton sts, T473-4403725, gdamuseum@gmail.com, Mon-Fri 0900-1630, Sat 1030-1300, EC$5/US$2,*

St George's

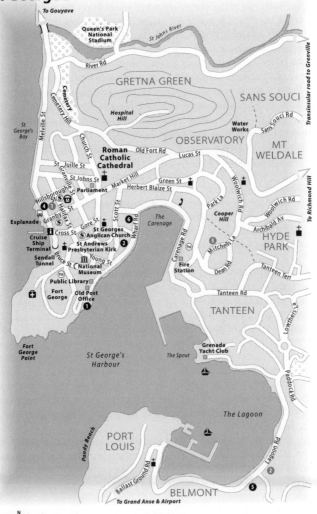

To Gouyave

Queen's Park National Stadium

St Johns River

River Rd

GRETNA GREEN

SANS SOUCI

Transinsular road to Grenville

St George's Bay

Cemetery Hill

Melville St

Cemetery

Church St

Hospital Hill

Water Works

Sans Souci Rd

MT WELDALE

OBSERVATORY

Old Fort Rd

Lucas St

Roman Catholic Cathedral

St Juille St

St Granville St

St Johns St

Parliament

Market Hill

Green St

Herbert Blaize St

Park La

Woolwich Rd

Woolwich Rd

To Richmond Hill

Hillsborough St

Halifax St

Granby St

Gore St

Scott St

Wharf Rd

The Carenage

Cooper Hill

Archibald Av

HYDE PARK

Esplanade

Cross St

St Georges Anglican Church

St Andrews Presbyterian Kirk

Young St

Mitchells La

Carenage Rd

Fire Station

Dean Rd

Tanteen Terr

Cruise Ship Terminal

Sendall Tunnel

Buce St

National Museum

Public Library

Fort George

Old Post Office

Tanteen Rd

TANTEEN

Lowthers La

Fort George Point

St George's Harbour

The Spout

Grenada Yacht Club

Paddock Rd

Pandy Beach

The Lagoon

PORT LOUIS

Ballast Ground Rd

BELMONT

Lagoon Rd

To Grand Anse & Airport

N

200 metres
200 yards

Where to stay
Deyna's City Inn 1
Tropicana 2
Visionview 3

Restaurants
BB's Crabback Caribbean 1
Creole Shack 6
Deyna's Tasty Foods 4

Nutmeg 2
Patrick's 5

just off the Carenage in the centre of town, is worth a visit. It used to be the **Antilles Hotel**, part of the former French barracks built in 1704. From 1767-1880, the British used parts as a prison, then the ground floor became a warehouse and upstairs a hotel. Note the cast iron balcony, not many of which are left in St George's. Displays cover a wide range of historical topics, pre-Columbian, natural history, colonial, military, Independence, the Cuban crisis, some items from West Africa, exhibits from the sugar and spice industries and of local shells and fauna. It isn't the grandest museum in the world but it is very informative and staff are helpful and knowledgeable. There is also a small café and on Friday evenings from 1730 there are cultural events such as drumming, singing, dancing, poetry and music concerts.

The **Public Library** is in a renovated old government building on the Carenage. In this part of the city are many brick and stone warehouses, roofed with red, fishtail tiles brought from Europe as ballast. A fire on 27 April 1990 damaged six government buildings on the Carenage, all now restored. Also on the Carenage is a monument to the **Christi Degli Abbissi**, or Christ of the Deep, moved from the entrance to the harbour, which commemorates 'the hospitality extended to the crew and passengers of the ill-fated liner', *Bianca C.* It stands on the walkway beside Wharf Road.

Fort George ① *US$2.* It is a very steep hike up the hill to this poorly maintained ruin, but it is well worth it. Dating from 1706, only the exterior walls are intact, and there is limited historical evidence except some dungeons, guard rooms and underground passages where bats now roost, but public viewpoints have been erected from which to see and take photos of the coast and harbour. Some old cannon are still in their positions and the views all round are tremendous. The French called it Fort Royale but the British named it Fort George. After the overthrow of Eric Gairy's government in 1979 it was briefly renamed Fort Rupert, but reverted to George after the return of democratic rule in 1983. There is a plaque marking the execution of Maurice Bishop in what is now a basketball court. Part of the property is used as the Police HQ.

Just down from the fort is **St Andrew's Presbyterian Kirk** (1830) also known as Scot's Kirk. Badly damaged by Hurricane Ivan, it is now being rebuilt together with reinforcement of the cliff wall to protect the entrance to the Sendall Tunnel as well as the church (www.presbyterianchurchgrenada.com).

Church Street and around On Church Street up the steep hill are a number of important buildings: **St George's Anglican Church** (1825), the **Roman Catholic Cathedral of the Immaculate Conception** (tower 1818, church 1884) and the **Supreme Court** and **Parliament** buildings (late 18th, early 19th century). St George's oldest religious building is the **Methodist Church**

European colonization and slavery

Aggressive defence of the island by the Kalinago (Caribs) prevented settlement by Europeans until the 17th century. In 1609 some Englishmen tried and failed, followed by a group of Frenchmen in 1638, but it was not until 1650 that a French expedition from Martinique landed and made initial friendly contact with the inhabitants. When relations soured, the French brought reinforcements and exterminated the Amerindian population. Sauteurs, or Morne des Sauteurs, on the north coast, is named after this episode when numerous Kalinago jumped to their death in the sea rather than surrender to the French.

The island remained French for about 100 years, although possession was disputed by Britain, and it was a period of economic expansion and population growth, as colonists and slaves arrived to grow tobacco and sugar at first, followed by cotton, cocoa and coffee. It was during the Seven Years' War in the 18th century that Grenada fell into British hands and was ceded by France to Britain as part of a land settlement in the 1763 Treaty of Paris. Although the French regained control in 1779, their occupation was brief and the island was returned to Britain in 1783 under the Treaty of Versailles. The British introduced nutmeg in the 1780s, after natural disasters wiped out the sugar industry. Nutmeg and cocoa became the main crops and encouraged the development of smaller land holdings. A major slave revolt took place in 1795, led by a free coloured Grenadian called Julien Fédon (see page 39), but slavery was not abolished until 1834, as in the rest of the British Empire.

(1820) on Green Street. Many of these buildings lost their roofs and sustained other damage from wind and rain during Hurricane Ivan in September 2004 and have still not been repaired. The Cathedral has been repaired, keeping the tower and the sanctuary, which were structurally sound, but demolishing the rest and replacing it with a steel structure and new roof. Sunday Mass is at 0800 and lasts two hours. The Anglican Church needs EC$2 mn as the roof fell in and the interior is nearly all destroyed, as are the parish buildings alongside, but it is fascinating to wander in and around the shell, reading the plaques that remain on the walls.

The Esplanade and around The Esplanade has been developed to take pressure off the Carenage. The cruise ship pier and terminal with shopping mall is here, the entry point for thousands of tourists. Further north is the main bus terminal and a car park, then the new fish market, all built on reclaimed land on the seaward side of the road. The **Market Square**, off Halifax Street (one of the

Independence

In 1833, Grenada was incorporated into the Windward Islands Administration which survived until 1958 when it was dissolved and Grenada joined the Federation of the West Indies. The Federation collapsed in 1962 and in 1967 Grenada became an associated state, with full autonomy over internal affairs, but with Britain retaining responsibility for defence and foreign relations. Grenada was the first of the associated states to seek full Independence, which was granted in 1974. Grenada is now an independent state within the Commonwealth, with the British monarch as Head of State represented by a Governor General. There are two legislative houses, the House of Representatives with 15 members, and the Senate with 13 members.

main streets, one steep block from the Esplanade), is always busy although the weekly market is on Saturday. There is a wide variety of local produce, herbs, spices and local crafts including luxuries such as nutmeg oil, nutmeg soap, rich cocoa balls, sold under cover. The trades people are keen to sell, but are polite, good-humoured and not pushy.

Queen's Park National Stadium Just north of the city is this stadium, rebuilt after Ivan with the help of the Chinese, which is used for all the main sporting activities, cricket, carnival shows and political events. The Chinese are now building a new football and athletics stadium.

Hyde Park Garden ① *Woolwich Rd, T473-4408395, www.hydeparkgrenada. com.* Keen gardeners should book a tour of this garden, situated on the hillside overlooking the lagoon and Port Louis Marina with views towards the city. Six generations of the Roberts family have lived here and the small estate is now in the hands of Fay Roberts Miller and her husband, John Miller, who between them have transformed former orchards and grazing land into one of the finest gardens in the Caribbean. The display of tropical flowers is so highly regarded that specimens are shipped to the Chelsea Flower Show in London each year to form part of the Grenada display, which invariably wins prizes. Tours are by appointment only, either directly by email with the owners or with an approved tour operator. The sunset tour is delightful and is followed by drinks on the veranda with the owners to take in the view and the colours.

Richmond Hill From Richmond Hill there are good views (and photo opportunities) of both St George's and the mountains of the interior. On

Revolution and US invasion

Political leadership after the 1950s alternated between Eric (later Sir Eric) Gairy's Grenada United Labour Party (GULP) and Herbert Blaize's Grenada National Party. At the time of Independence, Sir Eric Gairy was Prime Minister, but his style of government was widely viewed as authoritarian and corrupt, becoming increasingly resented by a large proportion of the population. In 1979 he was ousted in a bloodless coup by the Marxist-Leninist New Jewel (Joint Endeavour for Welfare, Education and Liberation) Movement, which formed a government headed by Prime Minister Maurice Bishop. Reforms were introduced and the country moved closer to Cuba and other Communist countries, who provided aid and technical assistance. In 1983, a power struggle within the government led to Bishop being deposed and he and many of his followers were murdered by a rival faction shortly afterwards. In the chaos that followed a joint US-Caribbean force invaded the island to restore order. They imprisoned Bishop's murderers and expelled Cubans and other socialist nationalities engaged in building an airport and other development projects.

Elections were held in 1984. They were won by the coalition New National Party (NNP), headed by Herbert Blaize, with 14 seats to GULP's one in the legislature. After the intervention, Grenada moved closer to the USA which maintains an embassy near the airport, but on 1 December 1999 diplomatic relations with Cuba were restored and embassies were opened in St George's and Havana.

In 1991 the Government decided to commute to life imprisonment the death sentences on 14 people convicted of murdering Maurice Bishop. Amnesty International and other organizations appealed for the release of Mrs Phyllis Coard, one of the 14 convicted, on grounds of ill-health following years of solitary confinement. She was allowed to go to Jamaica for cancer treatment in 2000, but was not pardoned. In 2006 the Truth and Reconciliation Commission released its long-awaited report about the events of October 1983, but it still left some questions unanswered. Herbert Blaize died in 1989 and Sir Eric Gairy in 1997.

the hill are Forts Matthew, Frederick and Adolphus, and the prison in which were held those convicted of murdering Maurice Bishop before Hurricane Ivan blew the roof off in 2004.

When the French defeated the British in 1779, they attacked from high ground inland rather than from the sea, which is what the British had expected. Fearing that the same might happen to them, the French built these forts with their cannon facing east, or inland, gaining them the nickname 'backwards facing forts'. However, a few years later, the island was returned to the British under the 1783 Treaty of Versailles, and the French never had time to finish their fortress building. Realizing their strategic importance, the British finished the job. Fort Frederick and Fort Adolphus were named after two sons of King George III, on the throne at the time; Fort Matthew was named after the island's governor, Edward Matthew, and a fourth, Fort Lucas, was named after the man from whom the French had acquired the land, William Lucas. **Fort Matthew** is the largest on the island and, although not open to the public, there are sometimes guided tours when you can see the 18th-century kitchen, bathrooms, cells used to restrain the insane and underground tunnels. **Fort Frederick** ① *entry US$2*, and from here there are spectacular views over St George's and the southern part of the island. It is sometimes used as a venue for weddings and other celebrations. The massive walls remain and there are some passages you can explore, but it is best to go with an informative guide to understand its significance.

Spice Basket ① *T473-4379000, www.spicebasketgrenada.com, open 0900-1700, EC$10.* In the residential area of Beaulieu is a complex including a theatre, pavillion, gift shop and two museums: the **Legacy Valley Museum**, tracing Grenada's history from pre-colonial times through to independence up to the present day, and the **West Indies Cricket Heritage Centre** (High Five), the world's first museum dedicated to the development of West Indies cricket. There is a huge display of cricket memorabilia including photos, bats, jackets, caps, match equipment, books and written records, curated by Phil Daniels.

East of St George's → *For listings, see pages 55-74.*

The Eastern Main Road heads east from Richmond Hill through numerous villages, twisting and turning, and there are a few places of interest for short excursions from St George's. In St Paul's is **de la Grenade Industries** ① *T473-4403241, www.delagrenade.com, Mon-Fri 0830-1530*, the business of la Grenade family, set up in the 1960s as a cottage industry by Sybil la Grenade and now run by her daughter, Cécile. The company is famous for its nutmeg jelly, nutmeg syrup and a host of sauces, syrups, beverages and preserves using local ingredients. Upgraded in 2009 with a good shop among its facilities, it also has a delightful Nutmeg Garden, covering two acres beside the factory. Here you can wander along paths of nutmeg shells among aromatic spices, herbs and fruit trees as well as flowering plants, all well-labelled, although there are also tour guides to explain plants' uses and pick fruit for you to try. You also get a good view of the Mount Gozeau Tropical Forest Reserve opposite the factory.

To see a good selection of Grenada's flowers and trees, ask whether the **Bay Gardens** at Morne Delice (turn off the Eastern Main Road at St Paul's police station, the gardens are on your left as you go down) have reopened. They were abandoned for a while but the family who own them are reported to be renovating again. It's a pleasant place; the paths are made of nutmeg shells and wind through a luxuriant jungle of plants including local fruits, herbs and spices.

If you take the next turning off the Eastern Main Road, just before the Texaco station, you reach the **Morne Gazo Nature Trails** ① *Mon-Sat 0900-1600, Sun 1000-1500, closed public holidays, EC$5, car park*, on your right. The conical Morne Gazo (or Delice Hill) rises to 1140 ft and the Forestry Department has created trails covered with nutmeg shells in the forest. At the summit a lookout platform gives a panoramic view of the island, down to the airport in the south, across to La Sagesse and up to the hills around Grand Étang. Information leaflets are available in several languages.

Further along the Eastern Main Road near Perdmontemps, is the turning for **Laura Spice and Herb Gardens** ① *T473-4432604, Mon-Fri 0830-1530, EC$5*, where you can see nutmeg, cloves and all the other spices and herbs grown on the island. A guide will give you a short tour of the property, explaining all the uses of the plants, and there is a small gift shop where you can buy spices. It is about 15 minutes' walk from a bus route.

Southwest Grenada → For listings, see pages 55-74.

Leaving St George's
From the Carenage, you can take a road which goes round the Lagoon, another sunken volcanic crater, now a yacht anchorage. This area is being developed with the construction of Port Louis (www.portlouisgrenada.com), a mixed-use resort and maritime community and a world-class marina for yachts up to 90 m. Still to come are houses, apartments, hotel, reclamation and renovation of the seafront and upgrading of Pandy Beach with provision of water sports and more sand.

Grand Anse
Carrying on to the southwest tip you come to Grand Anse, Grenada's most famous beach. Along its length are many hotels, but none dominates the scene since, by law, no development may be taller than a coconut palm. Access to the beach and parking is at Camerhogue Park at the north end by the **Spiceland** shopping mall.

Beaches on Grenada

There are 45 beaches on Grenada. The best are in the southwest, particularly Grand Anse, a lovely stretch of white sand which looks north to St George's. It can get crowded with cruise passengers, but there's usually plenty of room for everyone. Beach vendors have a proper market with booths, washroom facilities, a tourist desk and a jetty for water taxis, to prevent hassling on the beach. Morne Rouge, the next beach going southwest, is more private, has good snorkelling and no vendors. There are other nice, smaller beaches around Lance aux Épines. The beaches at Levera and Bathway in the northeast are also good, wild and unimproved.

Beaches and bays on the peninsula

From Grand Anse the road crosses the peninsula to a roundabout, from where roads lead off to the Point Salines Airport or the Lance aux Épines headland. The road to Portici and **Parc à Boeuf** beaches leads to the right, off the airport road. **Portici Beach** has good swimming despite a steeply shelving beach and excellent snorkelling around **Petit Cabrits point** at its northeast end. The next road to the right leads to **Magazine Beach**, then comes **Pink Gin Beach** and, practically as far as you can go, is the all-inclusive **Sandals** (formerly **La Source**), all very close to the airport.

On the south side of the peninsula, at **Prickly Bay** (the west side of Lance aux Épines) are hotels, the Spice Island Marina and other yachting and water sports facilities. Luxury homes take up much of **Lance aux Épines** down to Prickly Point. There is a glorious stretch of fine white sand where the lawns of the **Calabash Hotel** run down to the beach. This hotel has a very nice bar and restaurant open to non-residents and steel bands often play here. The next bay west, **True Blue Bay**, is smaller and quieter, with no real beach, but also has a hotel and yachting facilities as well as St George's University (www.sgu.edu) with its very popular School of Medicine that attracts many North American students.

Lower Woburn and around

From the Point Salines/Lance aux Épines roundabout you can head east along a road which snakes around the south coast. At Lower Woburn, a small fishing community (bus from St George's), you can see vast piles of conch shells in the sea, forming jetties and islets where they have been discarded by generations of lambi divers. Stop at **Island View Restaurant** or a local establishment, **Nimrod's Rum Shop**. Yachtsmen used to visit this spot to sign the infamous guest register and to be initiated with a shot of potent Jack Iron rum, but Hurricane Ivan blew away many of the log books. The local food is still good, though. You can go kayaking from Whisper Cove Marina on a variety of routes around Woburn Bay and out to Hog Island or Calivgny Island, checking out mangroves, with Conservation Kayak (www.conservationkayak.com).

Past Lower Woburn is the **Clarkes Court Rum Distillery** ⓘ *T473-4445363, www.clarkescourtrum.com, office and factory hours Mon-Fri 0800-1600, hospitality centre may open weekend and public holidays,* where 15-minute tours are available followed by rum tasting and sales at the hospitality centre. It is a steam-driven operation, unlike the river Antoine water-wheel system and old steam engines can be seen, the oldest dating from 1886. There has been a sugar mill on the estate since the 18th century and this factory dates from 1937, although no sugar has been crushed here since 2003 and molasses are now imported.

Southeast Grenada → *For listings, see pages 55-74.*

Any number of tracks and paths go inland to join the Eastern Main Road, or run along the rias and headlands, such as Calivgny, Fort Jeudy, Westerhall Point or La Sagesse with its nature reserve. Many of Grenada's most interesting and isolated bays are in the southeast, accessible only by jeep or on foot; taxis can drop you off at the start of a path and pick you up later.

La Sagesse Protected Seascape is a peaceful refuge which includes beaches, a mangrove estuary, a salt pond and coral reefs. In the coastal woodland are remains of sugar milling and rum distilleries. To get there turn south off the main road from St George's to Grenville opposite an old sugar mill, then take the left fork of a dirt road through a banana plantation. Close to the pink plantation house (see Where to stay), a few feet from a superb sandy beach, is **La Sagesse** bar and restaurant, good food, nutmeg shells on the ground outside. Walk to the other end of the beach to where a path leads around a mangrove pond to another palm-fringed beach, usually deserted. The snorkelling and swimming is good and there is a reef just offshore.

West coast Grenada → *For listings, see pages 55-74.*

The beautiful west coast road from St George's hugs the shore all the way to Duquesne Bay in the north with lovely views.

North to Halifax
Heading north out of St George's, past Queen's Park Stadium and **Grand Mal Bay**, you can turn inland to see petroglyphs, or rock carvings, near **Hermitage** (look for a sign on the road). **Beauséjour Estate**, once the island's largest, is now in ruins (except for the estate Great House). It is private, but from the road

you can see the remains of the sugar mill and distillery on the opposite side of the road from the sports ground.

If you turn inland at Beauséjour through rural countryside, you come to **Jessamine Eden** ① *Grenville Vale Rd, T473-2311501, www.jessamine-eden. com, daily 0900-1600, US$10*, a 60-acre estate, much of which is a botanical garden and through which flow rivers and streams. The entry fee allows you to wander freely along the trails which are pretty but, as few plants are labelled, the experience can be unedifying. It is better to make a reservation and get a guided tour of the gardens and the apiary with the owner, a research scientist. The organic honey and beeswax products are excellent. Spa treatments are also available and there is a very good restaurant featuring ingredients from the estate such as river crayfish.

Beyond Beauséjour is **Halifax Bay**, a beautiful, sheltered harbour, and the second most protected harbour in Grenada. It is interesting geologically as it is the remains of a volcanic crater which erupted some 15,000 years ago. It was settled first by Amerindians before being taken over by colonial planters and was also popular with smugglers. Looking back over Halifax harbour is an old plantation house, **Woodford Estate**, a wooden building with pretty tiles but unfortunately falling apart.

Concord to Fédon's Camp

At Concord, a road runs up the valley through nutmeg, cocoa, cashew, guava and clove trees to the **first Concord Falls** (45-minute hot walk from the main road or go by car, driving slowly, children and vendors everywhere). It is very busy at the end of the road with tour buses and spice stalls. There are toilets and changing facilities (small fee) if you want to bathe in the small cascade, but there is not much water in the dry season. Access is easy via steps with hand rails. The **second Concord Falls** (Au Coin) are bigger and higher, a 45- to 60-minute walk (each way), with a river to cross seven times (the bridges were never replaced after Hurricane Ivan washed them away, so be prepared to get wet feet); there is no need for a guide but it is advisable as much of the trail is overgrown. The **third falls** (Fontainebleu) is the hardest to get to and a guide is a good idea. It has a 65-ft cascade down the cliff face into a pool. Swimming is not allowed above the first falls as the water is part of the island's domestic water supply and you will see a small dam which diverts the flow.

Many hours further uphill is **Fédon's Camp**, at 2509 ft, where Julien Fédon (see box, opposite) fortified a hilltop in 1795 to await reinforcements from Martinique to assist his rebellion against the British. After fighting, the camp was captured; today it is a historical landmark. The trail to Fédon's Camp was badly damaged by Hurricane Ivan and has since become very overgrown. Fallen trees have not been cleared and passage is extremely difficult. You will need a guide with excellent local knowledge. Telfer Bedeau is the expert,

Julien Fédon, revolutionary and folk hero

Julien Fédon was the first revolutionary on Grenada and has become something of a folk hero, influencing nationalist leaders and later revolutionaries. He was the leader of a slave revolt in Grenada between 2 March 1795 and 19 June 1796, around the time that other rebellions were flaring up in other Caribbean islands such as Cuba and Jamaica. He was born on Martinique, the son of a French jeweller and a freed black slave, but the family moved to Grenada in the 1750s when the island was under French control. Fédon was influenced by ideology surrounding the French and Haitian Revolutions and his aim in the 1790s was to abolish slavery, to get rid of British rule and make Grenada a black republic. He set out with a force of about 100 freed slaves, attacking and killing British settlers in Gouyave

and Grenville, looting and burning their houses. He then retreated to the mountains of Belvedere where the rebels were joined by runaway slaves who had escaped from their plantations and they established several fortifications against the British retaliation. It is believed that about half the 28,000 slaves on Grenada at the time were allied to the revolutionary forces, together with many resident French citizens who wanted to get the island back to French control. On 8 April 1796, Fédon's brother was killed in action. To avenge his death, Fédon executed 48 prisoners, including Governor Ninian Home. The British regrouped with reinforcements and attacked the rebels on the steep slopes of Mount Qua Qua, many of whom threw themselves down the mountain rather than risk capture. Fédon was never found.

T437-4426200 (leave a message and he'll call you back), or you could try Justin Modeste (Gurry), from Gouyave, T473-4159311, who may be able to put you in touch with someone if he can't take you himself. It is possible to hike from Concord to Grand Étang in five hours; it's a hard walk, but rewarding. The trail is hard to spot where it leaves the path to the upper falls about two-thirds of the way up on the left across the river.

Dougaldston Estate

North of Concord, just before Gouyave (pronounced *Gwarve*), is a turn-off to Dougaldston Estate. Turn right just before a wide bridge, opposite a playing field. When the road bends to the right, go straight on and look for a gate on your left. It looks derelict. Before the revolution 200 people were employed here, cultivating spices and other crops. Now there are only a handful, the place is run down, the buildings in disrepair, the vehicles wrecked, but you can walk round and see the old machinery and imagine how it used to be. There is a wonderful

Kirani James

Kirani James, from Gouyave, is the first Grenadian to win an Olympic medal in any sport, having won gold at the 2012 London Olympics in the 400 m. A prodigious runner, specializing in both the 200 m and 400 m, he burst onto the headlines when, aged 14, he ran the fastest time ever by a boy of his age: 46.96 secs over 400 m at the 2007 World Youth Championship. He then went on to be the first boy to win the double 200 m/400 m at the 2009 World Youth Championships, smashing records in his wake. At least 10 colleges in the USA competed to offer him places, but he accepted a scholarship at Alabama, where he improved on his personal best times and set new college records. He continued to impress once he moved into adult competition, winning the 400 m at the 2011 World Championships in South Korea with a personal best of 44.60 secs, aged 18, making him the youngest ever 400-m world champion and

the first Grenadian to bring home a medal from a World Championship games. Shortly afterwards he improved his personal best with a time of 44.36 secs at the 2011 IAAF Diamond League in Zurich, winning gold again. His triumph at the 2012 London Olympics was achieved with a time of 43.94, making him the first non-US runner to break the 44-sec barrier. On his return home he was showered with plaudits; the government issued a commemorative stamp in his honour, named the new stadium after him, appointed him a tourism ambassador and awarded him bonds valued at EC$500,000. Since then he has continued to improve, clocking a winning time of 43.74 secs in the 400 m at the IAAF Diamond League Lausanne 2014. At the Commonwealth Games held in Glasgow in 2014, James set a new Commonwealth record of 44.24 secs and won Grenada's first ever Commonwealth Gold Medal.

view from the old estate house on the hill. Hurricane Ivan destroyed 80% of the nutmeg trees and 60-70% of cocoa bushes on the island and, although there has been a huge renovation programme, many are still covered in vines. At Dougaldston they still dry spices in the traditional way on racks which are wheeled under the building if it rains and someone will explain all the spices to you. However, there is no fermentation here now and the family has turned to tourism rather than agriculture. Staff are helpful and knowledgeable and will sell you bags of cinnammon, cloves or nutmeg, or there are mixed bags.

Gouyave

Gouyave, 'the town that never sleeps', is a fishing port, nutmeg collecting point and capital of St John's parish (http://gogouyave.gd). There are a few interesting old buildings; the post office, just past the shiny red fire engine, has an iron balcony. At the **Nutmeg Processing Station** ⓘ *a tour for US$2/EC$5 is highly recommended*, you can see all the stages of drying, grading, separating the nutmeg and mace and packing (give a tip). On the top floor mace is dried for four months in Canadian pine boxes before being graded. There are three grades, used for culinary spice, corned beef or cosmetics, and only Grenada produces grade one mace for cooking. On the first floor, nutmeg is dried on racks for two months, turned occasionally with a rake. The lighter ones are then used in medicine and the heavier ones for culinary spices. The husks are used for fuel or mulch and the fruit is made into nutmeg jelly (a good alternative to breakfast marmalade), syrup or liquor. The station is a great wooden building by the sea, with a very powerful smell. No photos are allowed. A little shop sells nutmeg products. There are two other nutmeg stations, at Victoria and Grenville, but they no longer process the nutmegs and simply collect them and send them to Gouyave for processing and export. There is also a nutmeg oil distillery at Sauteurs.

Gouyave is the principal place to go to for the **Fisherman's Birthday** festival. On Fridays from 1600, Gouyave is open to tourists on a grand scale, in the evening the main street is closed to traffic, there is seafood, drink and music and dancing.

Victoria and Tufton Hall Waterfall

North of Gouyave is **Victoria**, a fishing village and main centre of St Mark's, the smallest parish on the island. Victoria is the starting point for one of the toughest hikes on the island up to the tallest waterfall on Grenada at 80 ft: **Tufton Hall Waterfall**. For the fit, the hike will take up to three hours, so it is an all-day adventure. Along the way you will see other waterfalls, pools, sulphur springs and dense undergrowth as you get deeper into the beautiful countryside. Wear good shoes that you don't mind getting wet as much of the hike is in the river or alongside it clambering over boulders and even some rock climbing with the aid of a rope (safety harnesses not included, insurance policies probably void). If you need help to negotiate the route, some local guides to try include Kris, T473-4038674, Fenton, T473-4570191 or Wello, T473-4173244. **Tufton Hall Estate** (www.tuftonhallingrenada.com) is part of Peter de Savory's expanding tourist development, with a luxury eco-spa due to open in 2014, in what has previously been an untouched part of the island. Beautiful, panoramic views will add to the desirability of the hillside resort.

The road continues around the northwest coast, turning inland at **Duquesne** (pronounced *Duquaine*) where there is beautiful grey sand and petroglyphs on the beach (not particularly clean because of fishing), before returning to the sea at **Sauteurs**, the capital of St Patrick's parish, on the north coast. There is a lovely wild beach with leaning palm trees as you approach along the coast road. The town is renowned as the site of the mass suicide of Grenada's last 40 Caribs, who jumped off a cliff rather than surrender to the French (see box, page 31). Leapers Hill is appropriately in the cemetery by the church, behind the school. Recently redeveloped, there is an interpretation centre with a model of a Carib village, washrooms and shops, while a board shows all the islands you can see looking out to the north. In March Sauteurs celebrates St Patrick's Day with a week of events, exhibits of arts and crafts and a mini street festival.

Helvellyn House ① *T473-4429252, lunch 1200-1500, best to make a reservation when there isn't a tour party booked*, is perched on a hill in lovely gardens often used as a lunch stop with a view of the Grenadines and the mountains inland. There is also a wild but pretty beach five minutes' walk down from the garden if you want a paddle before or after lunch, or you can relax in a hammock and admire the flowers with Carriacou in the distance. At the side of the drive up to the house is an artisanal **pottery workshop** ① *Mon-Sat 0900-1700*, developed with the help of a Moroccan potter and still with a strong North African influence. The first designs were all Moroccan, but they have developed local themes and now use only local clay.

Morne Fendue plantation house is just south of Sauteurs and another popular place for tour groups to stop for lunch. The house was built in 1912 and still has all the old mouldings, cornices and light fittings of that time. It contains memorabilia dedicated to the previous owner, the late Betty Mascoll, MBE, a Grenadian nurse in the Second World War who was decorated by the Queen for her services to the community. The buffet lunch features local specialities and is served in an open-air dining room in front of the old colonial house built by Betty's mother with a view of Mount St Catherine. Reservations essential, T473-4429330.

East coast Grenada → *For listings, see pages 55-74.*

Levera

In the northeast, 450 acres around **Levera Pond** was opened as a national park in 1994. As well as having a bird sanctuary and sites of historic interest, Levera is one of the island's largest mangrove swamps; the coastal region has coconut palms, cactus and scrub, providing habitat for iguana and land crabs. There are

Grenada's birds

The endemic Grenada dove (*Leptotila wellsi*), the national bird, inhabits scrubby woodland, but is critically endangered. In 2007 an amendment to the National Parks Act allowed the sale of the Mount Hartmann National Park, the last stronghold of the dove, for the construction of a large tourist resort. About 120 birds, or half the total population, were believed to live in the area. In 2011 the government approved the protection of 100 acres of crown lands at the Beauséjour Estate adjacent to the Perseverance Protected Area and Dove Sanctuary, by which time the dove population was believed to have fallen to 132 birds.

In the rainforest you can see the emerald-throated hummingbird, yellow-billed cuckoo, red-necked pigeon, ruddy quail-dove, cocoa thrush and other species. Wading and shore birds can be spotted at Levera and in the south and southwest. The endangered and protected Grenada hook-billed kite (a large hawk, *Chondrohierax uncinatus mirus*) is found in the Levera National Park and in forested areas where there are mature trees. It uses its beak to pluck tree snails (its only food) out of their shells. A pile of shells with holes is evidence that a kite ate there. There are believed to be only about 50-75 Grenada hook-billed kites left on the island. Habitat destruction is its greatest threat, whether by hurricanes or construction of tourist resorts and residences.

white beaches where turtles lay their eggs and, offshore, coral reefs and the Sugar Loaf, Green and Sandy islands. You can swim at Bathway but currents are strong at other beaches. The coast between Levera Beach and Bedford Point is eroding rapidly, at a rate of several feet a year. To get here from Sauteurs a road approaches **Levera Bay** from its west side. Turn left at **Chez Norah's** bar, a two-storey green corrugated-iron building (snacks available); the track rapidly becomes quite rough and the final descent to Levera is very steep, suitable only for 4WD. A better way to Levera approaches from the south. The road forks left about two miles south of Morne Fendue, passes through river Sallee and past Bathway Beach.

The **River Sallee Boiling Springs** are an area of spiritual importance; visitors are inspired to throw coins into the fountain while they make a wish. There are six holes, which bubble at a temperature of 35°C. The largest is brown and muddy but the other five are clear and salty, despite being about a mile from the sea.

Bathway Beach is a popular weekend spot when it can get busy. It is a huge dark golden stretch of sand, with cliffs at either end, trees for shade, a beach bar, snack bars, picnic tables, a few vendors and the **Levera National Park** visitors' centre. Some small shops were built in 2014. There is a ridge of rocks just offshore, parallel with the beach, which provides protection for swimming, almost like a swimming pool, but you must not swim beyond the rocks or you will be drowned.

From here a dirt road leads past **Levera Pond**, which is gradually recovering from Hurricane Ivan. The 22-acre freshwater pond is surrounded by mangroves and is an important wetland, attracting migratory and resident birds, including the scarlet ibis (*Eudocimus ruber*). Birds are best seen early morning or late evening.

A trail leads from the track between Bathway Beach and Levera Beach to a viewing platform. Swimming is good at the beautiful and wild **Levera Beach** where leatherback turtles come to nest in April to June, and there is surf in certain conditions. It is not as busy as Bathway because not many people want to subject their vehicles to the dusty/muddy, potholed, dirt road. Do not swim far out as there is a current in the narrows between the beach and the privately owned **Sugar Loaf Island**. Boat trips go out to the island, which is good for snorkelling. You can arrange a taxi service with local fishermen. East of Sugar Loaf Island are Green Island and Sandy Island.

South of Levera

South of Levera the coastal road runs to **Lake Antoine**, another crater lake, but sunken to only about 20 ft above sea level; it has been designated a Natural Landmark. Like St George's and Grand Étang, the water has risen at times of volcanic activity, notably in 1902.

Nearby is the **River Antoine Rum Distillery** ① *T473-4427109, US$2/EC$5, guided tours,* driven by a water mill, the oldest in the Caribbean, the paddle wheel was installed in 1785. Grinding of the sugar cane is done in the mornings and the basic distillation process results in the Rivers Royale Grenadian Rum, which at 75% alcohol is breathtaking firewater. However, if the water level is low (in dry season) the waterwheel can't turn, they can't grind sugar cane and consequently they can't make rum. At the distillery there is also the Rivers Restaurant and Bar.

Dunfermline Rum Distillery can also be visited. There are no actual tours but the staff will show you around. The rum here is bottled at 70° proof.

Belmont Estate

① *T473-4429524, www.belmontestate.net, Sun-Fri, 0800-1600, tours from 0800 EC$13, lunch 1200-1430 EC$48 plus service and VAT, Bean to Bar tour of estate, Grenada Chocolate Company and lunch EC$175.*

Inland is this estate, which dates from the 17th century. It is now a major agritourism attraction, a working cocoa and nutmeg plantation with tours of the organic farm, goat dairy farm (http://thegoatdairy.org), gardens, heritage museum and cocoa processing facilities. You can tour the 400-acre estate and follow the cocoa beans from bush to export. At the boucan, you see the

Ivan the Terrible

September 2004 was the month no Grenadian will forget, when Hurricane Ivan passed directly over the island, killing 37 people, damaging or destroying practically every building and leaving 50,000 homeless. Water, electricity and phone services were cut off, looting was rife and a dawn to dusk curfew was imposed with the help of regional security services, who were also drafted to help guard prisoners after the prison had its roof blown off. It took several weeks for power to be restored, but shortages of food and building supplies continued for months, with many homes unrepaired for lack of materials. Most hotels were soon open for business, even if some rooms were still out of action, although some took the opportunity for an extended closure to carry out improvements and upgrading. By the winter season, cruise ships were calling again and the airport was back to normal. Today there is still some evidence of the hurricane's passing. Apart from the church roofs still missing and the tree stumps in the forest, houses are more visible without the trees which used to obscure them and residents feel that their neighbours are closer than they realized.

cocoa being fermented and other agricultural processes such as the cleaning of mace. The heritage museum is complemented by shows of traditional activities such as stick fighting, nation drumming, bele and pique dancing and games once practised by the slaves. A buffet lunch at the restaurant uses all local ingredients, including goats' cheese, cocoa, fruit and vegetables as well as serving local specialities such as callaloo and pepperpot.

The nutmeg trees were badly damaged when Hurricane Ivan trashed everything in its wake, slashing production on Grenada by 75 per cent. Cocoa has now replaced nutmeg as the main crop, helped by the establishment of the **Grenada Chocolate Company**, a mile away at Hermitage. Producers here and on other farms were encouraged to go organic and offered a guaranteed price for their beans. Sadly, the founder, Mott Green, died in 2013, but the company and a tourism collaboration with Belmont Estate continue to flourish. Tours of the factory can be done as part of the 'bean to bar' tour offered by Belmont Estate (reservations required). Using certified organic cocoa beans from local growers and organic sugar imported from a cooperative in Paraguay, this tiny factory roasts and grinds all its own beans and produces some of the world's finest chocolate. The whole operation is solar powered and the shells and dust are recycled as fertilizer around the cocoa bushes. Staff will explain and show you the manufacturing process, and you can buy their delicious organic chocolate or cocoa powder/drinking chocolate for cocoa tea. **The Bonbon Shop** on Belmont Estate sells the bars of chocolate and also delicious truffles

Janet House

Around Grenada you will see small wooden shacks clinging to their existence, perched on concrete pillars at each corner. These prefabricated homes made of timber imported from Suriname were put up after the passage of the devastating hurricane Janet in 1955, which swept through Grenada and the Grenadines before making landfall in Mexico. Designed as homes for the poor and homeless after the storm, corruption meant that many made their way into the hands of richer people who used them for different purposes. Being made of shiplap timber, they also housed bed bugs and other unwanted creatures and, if you took them down and reassembled them elsewhere, they never fitted together quite the same and there would be gaps in the walls. Over the years their owners have customized them, but the basic structure remains the same.

flavoured with local spices. The pure chocolate will not melt in the car on the way home and survives island hopping or transatlantic flights perfectly! It can also be bought in the UK at Waitrose.

To get there turn towards Sauteurs when you reach the Tivoli/La Poterie junction near Tivoli Roman Catholic church; at the next junction turn left and Belmont is on your right after a minute or so.

Pearls Airport

Amerindian remains can be seen at an archaeological dig near the old Pearls Airport. Apparently it's so unprotected that lots of artefacts have been stolen. The airport is worth a quick visit to see the two old Cuban and Russian planes and the duty-free shop, a ghost town, although the runway is well used for driving lessons, cricket, biking, go-karting and social encounter in general.

Grenville

Grenville, also known by its old French name, La Baye, or dubbed Rainbow City, is the main town on the east coast and capital of St Andrew's Parish. This is the largest parish in Grenada with a population of about 25,000, although the town has only about 2400 residents. It is a collection point for bananas, nutmeg and cocoa, and also a fishing port. There are some well-preserved old buildings, including the Court House, Anglican Church, police station and post office. Good local food can be found here along the main street, try **Ebony's** for roti, curry mutton, stewfish, Creole fish and rice and peas, or **Rins**, right by the buses to town, which is the best place for roti. The **Rainbow City Festival** is held here at the start of August, coinciding with Emancipation Day festivities, with arts and crafts displays, street fairs and food, cultural shows and drumming.

Marquis Falls and Island

Two miles south of Grenville are the **Marquis Falls**, also called Royal Mount Carmel Falls. The combined height of the two drops make the waterfall among the highest in Grenada. At the bus shelter by the sign for the falls on the road you can usually find a local guide if you want one. There have been complaints of hassling but there is no compulsion for you to hire anyone. It is an easy 10- to 15-minute walk from the road unless it has been raining, when it becomes muddy and slippery on the trail and a guide can be helpful for the less able. You can take a dip in the pool downstream and a power shower in the waterfalls. There is a natural water slide and some people like to jump off the rocks into the pool where it is deep enough to swim. Water shoes are a good idea as the rocks are slippery. Marquis village was the capital of St Andrew's in the 17th and 18th centuries. Nowadays it is the centre of the wild pine handicraft industry.

Marquis Island, off the east coast, can be visited; at one time it was part of the mainland and now has eel grass marine environments and coral reefs. Nearby is **La Baye Rock**, which is a nesting ground for brown boobies, habitat for large iguanas and has dry thorn scrub forest. It too is surrounded by coral reefs.

The interior → *For listings, see pages 55-74.*

The high forest receives over 160 ins of rain a year. Epiphytes and mosses cling to the tree trunks and many species of fern and grasses provide a thick undergrowth. The trees include the gommier, bois canot, Caribbean pine and blue mahoe. At the summit, the vegetation is an example of elfin woodland, the trees stunted by the wind, the leaves adapted with drip tips to cope with the excess moisture.

Mount St Catherine

This peak is the highest point on the island, at 2756 ft. It is the youngest of the five volcanos that make up the island and has a horseshoe-shaped crater open to the east with several lava domes in it. There are two routes up, one from Victoria but perhaps easiest from Grenville. Take a minibus to the Mount Hope road, this is a 4WD track which becomes the path up the mountain. It takes at least two hours from leaving the minibus. A guide is not necessary but is recommended. Do not go alone, however, and do not go at all if you suffer from vertigo. Don't take chances with daylight either. Parts of the trail are very steep and muddy and there can be landslips in wet weather. Wear good hiking shoes that will withstand copious mud. For information on this and anything else, contact Mr and Mrs Benjamin at **Benjamin's Variety Store** ⓘ *Victoria St, Grenville, T473-4426200*. Mrs Benjamin is on the Tourist Board. Telfer Bedeau, from Soubise, is the hiking expert and Mrs Benjamin can put you in touch with him.

Telfer Bedeau

Now in his seventies, Telfer Bedeau is still the best hiking guide on Grenada and proud owner of the British Empire Medal for his guiding and charity work. Based in Soubise, near Grenville, he knows the forest and mountain trails around the island better than anyone else and leads visiting hikers up Mount Catherine like a mountain goat – twice a day if necessary. He does not have a car and prefers to take his clients around the island by bus, giving them not only an intimate perspective of the island's culture but also the freedom to start and finish hikes wherever he chooses. Bedeau is not only a guide, but also a naturalist, adventurer and raconteur. He has rowed, windsurfed and kayaked around Grenada; in his younger days he worked on local boats, including the smuggling run from St-Barts and knows the sea almost as well as the land. The stories of his life blend with his discourses on local plant life and their medicinal uses giving the visitor brain stimulation to go with the physical work-out of keeping up with him. Although now a local celebrity, recognized everywhere, Bedeau remains modest and charming, a true gentleman.

The transinsular, or hill road, from Grenville to St George's used to be the route from the Pearls Airport to the capital, which all new arrivals had to take. It is well surfaced, but twisty and narrow. The minibus drivers on it are generally regarded as 'maniacs', one bend is called 'Hit Me Easy'. The road rises up to the rainforest, often entering the clouds. If driving yourself, allow up to 1½ hours from Levera to St George's.

St Margaret and Seven Sisters Falls

Shortly before reaching the Grand Étang (see page 49), there is a side road to the St Margaret, or **Seven Sisters Falls**. The two falls at the end of the trail are very beautiful and you can have a refreshing swim in the pool at the base. They are only a 30-minute walk from the main road, but a guide can be useful if you are likely to need assistance on the tricky bits of the trail, such as the steep downhill part before you get to the falls where there are muddy steps and boulders to negotiate.

Honeymoon Falls About 20 minutes further upstream are the delightful Honeymoon Falls, a wet and rather tricky scramble over boulders and rocks and through cascades. The trail runs over private land, so a small fee of EC$5/ US$2 is payable to the owners who keep the paths clear, at their booth by the main road where there is a tiny car park. Hiking sticks are available to borrow, which are recommended. Your guide will probably dive in off the rocks to entertain you. A tip is, of course, expected for his services.

Grand Étang National Park and Forest Reserve

ⓘ *Sun-Fri 0800-1600, US$2, interpretation centre overlooking the lake has exhibitions and leaflets about the trails, bar, shop, toilets.*

The focal point of Grenada's nature tourism lies eight miles from the capital in the central mountain range. It is right on the transinsular road. The Grand Étang is a crater lake surrounded by lush tropical forest. A series of trails has been blazed which are well worth the effort for the beautiful forest and views, but can be muddy and slippery after rain. The **Morne Labaye** nature trail is only 15 minutes long, the return is along the same route; the shoreline trail around the lake takes 1½ hours and is moderately easy; much further, 1½ hours' walk away, is **Mount Qua Qua**, from which you get expansive and beautiful views. The path is well travelled but as usual parts can get muddy after rain. The trail then continues for an arduous three hours to **Concord Falls**, with an extra 30-minute spur to **Fédon's Camp** (see page 38). This trail is difficult as bridges have been washed away and parts are overgrown or destroyed by mudslides. Be prepared for razor grass and clouds of mosquitoes. Walking sticks are a help. Take food and water. From Concord Falls it is 25 minutes' walk to the road to get a bus to St George's.

After Grand Étang, there is a **viewpoint** at 1910 ft overlooking St George's. A bit further down the hill is a detour to the pretty **Annandale Falls** which plunge about 40 ft into a pool where the locals dive and swim. Foreigners can too, but most people just walk to the viewing platform and don't stop long. Tourists are pestered for money here, for diving, singing, information, trinkets, whether requested or not. It is on the cruise ship tour circuit and suffers as a result. If coming from St George's on Grenville Road, fork left at the Methodist Church about half way to Grand Étang.

The peaks in the southeast part of the Grand Étang Forest Reserve can be walked as day trips from St George's. For **Mount Maitland** (1712 ft), take a bus from the Market Place to Mardigras, or if there is none, get off at the junction at St Paul's and walk up. At the Pentecostal (IPA) church, turn left and immediately right. The paths are reasonably clear and not too muddy as 4WD vehicles have to get up to service the antennae on the top. The walk takes less than one hour each way. There are excellent views from the top over both sides, with some hummingbirds.

Mount Sinai (2306 ft) is not as spectacular as Mount St Catherine, nor as beautiful as Mount Qua Qua, but is not as muddy either. Take a bus to Providence, then walk up (two hours) the particularly lovely road to Petit Étang and beyond, where the road turns into a track in the banana fields. The path up the mountain begins behind a banana storage shed and must be closely watched. The terrain is a bit tricky near the top. There is a path down the other side to Grand Étang. Local opinions vary as to how badly you would get lost without a guide as the paths are no longer maintained.

Carriacou → *For listings, see pages 55-74.*

Carriacou (pronounced Carrycoo), named Kayryouacou by the Caribs, which means 'island of reefs', is an attractive island of green hills descending to sandy beaches. It is less mountainous than Grenada, which means that any cloudy or rainy weather clears much quicker. Sailing boats and fishing have traditionally been the mainstay of life on Carriacou and boat building is part of the culture, being celebrated in festivals and regattas throughout the year. Efforts are being made by the Government to curb contraband and drug smuggling in Carriacou, but a lot comes in around Anse la Roche, where there are picturesque smugglers' coves.

Arriving in Carriacou
Getting there There are flights from Barbados and Grenada in small planes, or you can get here by sea on a hovercraft, large ferries for cargo and passengers or yacht. It is a lovely route, following the length of Grenada's western coastline before crossing the channel to Carriacou and seeing the Grenadines coming into view. On the crossing look out for dolphins which follow the boats. The *Osprey* hovercraft is recommended as being the most reliable service and the boat is in good condition. In heavy seas you may get seasick on any boat, said to be worse going to Carriacou than coming back. ▸▸ *See Transport, page 74, for further details.*

Getting around Minibuses run to most parts of the island and will convert to a taxi to take you off route. Car hire is available, which is useful if you are staying in self-catering accommodation and need to shop. Cycling is recommended, the traffic is very light. Many of the roads are in very poor repair, giving the semblance of off-road cycling, although some of the main roads have recently been repaved. There is potential for lots of flat tyres in the dry season as there is an abundance of cacti. Walking is equally rewarding, the heat being the main problem. There is good walking on the back roads and the woods are teeming with wildlife such as iguanas. Some beaches can only be reached on foot or by boat. Water taxis are on hand to take you to beaches in remote parts of the island, or to the islets offshore for picnics and snorkelling.

Places in Carriacou
Hillsborough Carriacou's capital has a population of about 1000. It dates from a colonial settlement towards the end of the 18th century and was used by

Admiral Ralph Abercrombie who came with 150 ships to launch an attack on the Spanish in 1796 and capture Trinidad. Main Street runs parallel to the sea and the hub of activity is the dock area where you find Customs, Immigration, Police, taxis, buses, and fruit and vegetable stalls. Also along Main Street there are guesthouses, a few restaurants, bars, a supermarket, shops, internet access, banks and a dive shop. The town is also blessed with a lovely beach, a huge curve of white sand with good swimming, despite the presence of the jetty and large cargo ships. Along Paterson Street are the telephone office, the tourist office and the small museum.

Carriacou Historical Society Museum ⓘ *T473-4438288, http://carriacou museum.org, Mon-Fri 0930-1600, Sat 1000-1600*, housed in an old cotton ginnery, has exhibits from Amerindian settlements in the island and from later periods in its history, including African artefacts, documents, furniture, household items and pottery (there's a small shop for gifts, cards, books and

Carriacou

N

1 km

1 miles

Where to stay 🛏
Bayaleau Point
Cottages **1**
Bogles Round House **2**

Carriacou Grand View **5**
Green Roof Inn **6**
Melodie's Guest House **3**

local music). The manager, Clemencia Alexander, is happy to explain the exhibits in a short guided tour. The museum is funded by donations, grants and membership fees, so anything you can give is much appreciated.

The people maintain a strong adherence to their African origins and the annual **Big Drum Dances**, which take place around Easter, as well as those performed at weddings, wakes, tombstone feasts, boat launches and community gatherings, are almost purely West African. French traditions are still evident at L'Esterre and there is a vigorous Scottish heritage, especially at **Windward**, where the people are much lighter skinned than elsewhere on the island. Windward used to be the centre for the craft of hand-built schooners but in recent years the boat builders have expanded to Tyrell Bay. Begun by a shipbuilder from Glasgow, the techniques are unchanged, but the white cedar used for the vessels is now imported from Grenada or elsewhere. The sturdy vessels are built and repaired without the use of power tools in the shade of the mangroves at the edge of the sea. To show the qualities of these local boats, the **Carriacou Regatta** was initiated in 1965, see page 18.

North of Hillsborough The **Anglican Rectory** is in what remains of the **Beausejour Great House**, on a slight hill so that the master could watch his slaves in the sugar and cotton fields below. The house is now single storey, having lost the second floor in Hurricane Janet in 1955. At **Belair National Park** by a nature centre and a forest reserve containing teak and mahogany, you

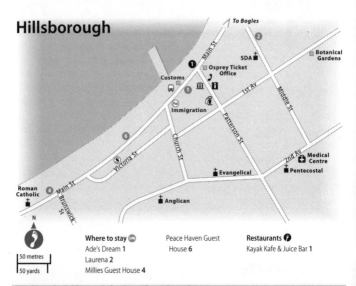

Hillsborough

To Bogles

Botanical Gardens

SDA

Osprey Ticket Office

Customs

Immigration

Main St

1st Av

Middle St

Patterson St

Church St

Victoria St

2nd Av

Medical Centre

Evangelical

Pentecostal

Roman Catholic

Main St

Brunswick St

Anglican

N

50 metres
50 yards

Where to stay
Ade's Dream **1**
Laurena **2**
Millies Guest House **4**

Peace Haven Guest House **6**

Restaurants
Kayak Kafe & Juice Bar **1**

can see the ruins of the old government house. The house was stripped bare during the US invasion of Grenada but the park is now used to hold the annual Maroon and String Band Music Festival. There are good trails through the park for a pleasant walk.

On Hospital Hill, Belair, northeast of Hillsborough, there is an **old sugar mill** with stunning views. The tower is well preserved, but not much else is left. The slaves had to carry the sugar cane all the way up the hill. The best views, however, are from the **Princess Royal Hospital** itself, built on top of the hill in 1907-1909 because of an outbreak of malaria. The wind up on the hill is too strong for mosquitoes and it was also considered a nice, quiet spot for patients to recuperate. From here you get a fabulous view of Hillsborough, and most of the southern part of the island. A few old cannons were put here in 1948. Under the flamboyant tree in the courtyard there are some large, bored tortoises (*morrocoy*).

South of Hillsborough The road runs along the coast through Coconut Grove (Hurricane Lenny washed the palms away in 1999) and across the airport runway to Paradise Beach and L'Esterre. **Paradise Beach** is one of the nicest beaches on the island, reached by bus (no: 10 from Hillsborough). The local painter, Canute Calliste (1914-2005), had his studio at **L'Esterre**. His naïve style captured the scenes of Carriacou. The road then cuts across the peninsula to **Harvey Vale**, at Tyrell Bay. Visitors should see the oyster beds at **Tyrell Bay** where 'tree-oysters' grow on mangrove roots. Tyrell Bay is an anchorage for yachts and the mangroves are a hurricane hole. There are a couple of good restaurants, popular with the yachting fraternity, attracted also by Carriacou Marine, which is a port of entry as well as chandlery and boatyard.

Sandy Island This island is a tiny, low-lying atoll in Hillsborough Bay off Lauriston Point, a sand spit with a few palm trees for shade and a bit of scrub. There is excellent swimming and snorkelling, but take an umbrella for shade, sunscreen, food and drink. You can get Joy's water taxi from **Hardwood Bar** on Paradise Beach, or Curtis from **Off the Hook Bar** may also take you in his boat, both of whom have snorkelling gear for rent, five minutes, EC$70/US$30 return for two people. You can also go by water taxi from Hillsborough EC$70, 30 minutes each way, or join a dive boat for an excursion with diving or snorkelling. The area is now a marine protected area to prevent cruise ships swamping the sand bank with 200 tourists at a time, damaging the reef with anchor chains. Now people come in small groups on small boats and stay for two or three hours allowing the vegetation and reef to recover. There are moorings for yachts, which have to pay a fee.

Alternatively, try **White Island**, a similar islet in Manchineel Bay, a mile off the south coast, fringed by sandy beaches except for a steep cliff face at one end. It is a private island and for sale in 2014 with permission to build a house on its 9 acres.

The north **Bogles** is the most northerly village on the west side of the island and the end of the concrete road. From here 4WD or at least high clearance is necessary in the wet season. The Bogles emporium is an old building at the junction of the road to Windward, built in the mid-19th century by a merchant. Although desperately in need of renovation, the top floor overhang still has the original iron supports, denoting prosperity at the time of construction.

A beautiful beach is **Anse La Roche**, which faces west and has a spectacular view across the strait to the mountains of rugged Union Island. Snorkelling is good, particularly among the rocks at the side. Take food and drink and no valuables of any sort; there are no facilities and few people. It is very easy to get lost walking to Anse La Roche beach and it is easier to take a water taxi there, although if you do walk, you're advised to take insect repellent. It's very peaceful, watch the yachts rounding the headland on their way to anchorage; at night turtles swim ashore to lay their eggs.

This end of the island has the highest elevation, **High North Peak**, which rises to 955 ft and is part of a protected area. **YWF-Kido Foundation and Ecological Research Station** ⓘ *T473-4437936, www.kido-projects.com and http://kidoplanet.com*, is near Anse La Roche and High North Park, where you can go birdwatching, hiking, cycling, whale watching and even volunteering for one of the conservation projects such as helping with turtle nesting season. Illegal sand mining and rising sea levels have reduced the area of beach above the high water mark, meaning that turtle nests can get flooded unless dug up and moved higher up by YWF-Kido staff. They have also campaigned for a total moratorium on hunting and killing of sea turtles, which still happens in Grenada. Founded by two Italian conservationists, the Foundation recruits volunteers locally and from abroad and is involved in local education as well as animal rescue and rehabilitation. Accommodation is available.

You can walk all round the north of the island. The British placed a cannon here in the 1780s. A path leads down (opposite a mauve-painted house) to the beach at **Petit Carenage Bay**, which has coarse, coral sand, good swimming and modest surf in some conditions. Returning to the road, Windward is a few minutes' walk further on, with a few shops and local bars. This old Scottish fishing and boat building village is the place where traditional sailing fishing vessels are still made. Take a bus there and go for a walk along the beach or further afield. The Caribbean coast is spectacular in places and a walk from Windward to Dover, then following the coast road until it becomes a dirt road leading to Dumfries, is very pleasant and secluded.

Petite Martinique is the only offshore island from Carriacou on which people live, descended from French fishermen, Glaswegian shipwrights, pirates and slaves. As a result of the French settlement, the population is mainly Roman Catholic and the Parish Priest is always the Council Chairman. Its area is 486 acres, rising to a small, volcanic peak, and only a very small channel separates it from Petit St Vincent, where many people work at the resort.

The principal legal occupations are boatbuilding and fishing, but for generations the islanders have been involved in smuggling and they are noticeably more prosperous than their neighbours. There was excitement in 1997 when the government proposed to build a house for 12 Coast Guard personnel in the campaign against drug smuggling. Half the population turned out to demonstrate against the arrival of government surveyors and clashed with armed police and the Special Services Unit.

The big event of the year is the **Whitsuntide Regatta Festival**, designed to foster competition between the fishing and sailing communities of Grenada, Carriacou and Petite Martinique as well as the Grenadines of St Vincent. There are many classes of boat races and lots of onshore competitions and activities too, including the greasy pole and tug of war.

There are a couple of guesthouses where you can stay and a good restaurant and bar, popular with the charter yacht business. Alternatively, if you come in by ferry, the restaurant will serve you lunch, then take you across to Petit St Vincent for a few hours on the beach there before bringing you back in time for the return ferry. They will also take you to the Mopion sandbank, but that takes longer to get to and therefore a better trip if you are staying overnight. There is a dock with fuel, water, ice and other yachting supplies. Water taxis are available from Windward on Carriacou. The *Osprey Express* and the mailboat call here after Hillsborough coming from St George's.

◉ Grenada listings

For hotel and restaurant price codes and other relevant information, see pages 13-16.

◉ Where to stay

St George's *p28, map p29*
$$$$ The Lodge, on the Morne Jaloux ridge ½ mile south of Forts Matthew and Frederick, T473- 4402330, www.thelodgegrenada.com. House dates from 1920s, built on site of older place, lots of character, high ceilings, old-style plantation house windows, wooden furniture made of blue mahoe. Intimate, with only 2 rooms with huge beds with nets, luxuriously furnished, 25-m rainwater-fed, chemical-free lane

pool, panoramic views of sunrise, sunset and mountains from garden terrace and veranda looking through spectacular passion fruit vine. Strictly vegan food with 3 meals a day offered, packages available. Great food using organic produce from hillside garden, chocolate puddings using **Grenada Chocolate Company** delights. Mark and his son, Matthew, are wonderful hosts and can arrange anything for you. The house was once the Venezuelan embassy and when the Americans invaded they didn't recognize the flag and thought it was Cuban; gunshot holes are still visible on the veranda.

$$$ Tropicana, Lagoon Rd, T473-4401586, www.tropicanainn.com. Pleasant small hotel, no frills, fridge, TV, a/c, balcony, small but adequate bathroom, high ceilings, view over water (except for triple room overlooking rear), some interconnect, nicest rooms on top floor, room service, restaurant and bar at street level open 0730-2400, good local breakast, Fri barbeque buffet, convenient for buses.

$$$ Visionview, Mitchell's Lane, www.visionview.webs.com. If you prefer to be self-catering, these 2 2-bedroom apartments offer all the requirements for independent living on hillside with a great view of the Carenage from the balcony. The bedrooms are small but there is a/c, decent kitchen and living area and airport transfers on request.

$$ Deyna's City Inn, Melville St, Esplanade, T473-4357007, cityinn@ spiceisle.com. For many years **Deyna's** has been the place to eat local food and now you can stay there too, popular with Caricom and low-budget visitors. Rooms are small but spotless and well furnished, with good a/c and excellent local breakfast to set you up for the day. Right on waterfront overlooking cruise ships and bus station so you're at the heart of the activity; don't expect peace and quiet but there's always something to watch from the balcony. Lunch and dinner at **Spices Restaurant and Bar** or the more informal **Deyna's Tasty Foods**, all on the property.

Southwest Grenada *p35, map p27*
$$$$ Blue Horizons, Grand Anse, T473-4444316, www.grenadablue horizons.com. Set back from beach, short walk, use of facilities at Spice Island, the sister hotel on beach. Tastefully decorated self-catering studios and suites with kitchenettes, some of which interconnect, parking, pool, pleasant grounds with intact mature, tall trees and palms attracting lots of birds, **La Belle Créole** restaurant is good.

$$$$ Calabash, Lance aux Épines, T4444334, www.calabashhotel.com. Suites and villas around an elegant central lawn with palm trees and flowering bushes leading down to the sea. This is one of the oldest and nicest hotels on the island with one of the loveliest settings and good beach. Pleasant and unpretentious, excellent service. Very comfortable, spacious, breakfast served on suites' large balconies, complimentary afternoon tea. Notable for its **Rhodes Restaurant**, open 1900-2130, headed by UK celebrity chef, Gary Rhodes (smart casual dress code), and it also has **Bash Restaurant by Mark B**, open 1130-1800, for tapas and light bites as well as lunch beachside open 1200-1500. Water sports, tennis, fitness room, computer/TV room.

$$$$ The Flamboyant, Grand Anse, T473-4444247, www.flamboyant.com. 60 units in standard or superior rooms, suites and cottages, at the south end of Grand Anse on hillside, lovely views, steep walk down to beach from upper rooms with best views, but transport for people with mobility problems to restaurant and beach, quite a walk to bus stop. Not luxury, but more than adequate; some rooms have kitchenettes. Food is good and they are helpful with special diets. The road goes through the property with gym, pool, restaurant and late-night sports bar at sea level and rooms above the road. **Dive Grenada** on site.

$$$$ Laluna, Morne Rouge, T437-4390001, www.laluna.com. Always highly rated, 1- or 2-bedroom colour-washed cottages and a 5-bedroom villa on 10 acres of hillside and beach at the end of the bay, private, height of luxury, open Italian/Indonesian minimalist style with Italian linens, drapes, furniture from Bali, shower with sea view, bath goodies from monastery in Italian Alps, private plunge pools on veranda. The main buildings on the beach are wooden and cement with thatched roofs around the main pool, dining room serving Italian and Thai food. Yoga, pilates, tai chi, meditation and massage on your veranda, complimentary mountain bikes,

snorkelling, hobie cats and kayaks. children under 10 not welcome in high season.

$$$$ Lance aux Épines Cottages, Lance aux Épines, T473-4444565, www.laecottages.com. Cottages and apartments set apart from each other in 3 acres of gardens right on the beach in walking distance of several restaurants and minimart, next to Calabash. Full kitchen, staff will shop and cook if you want, or show you how to make local specialities, all exceptionally helpful, spacious rooms, quarry tiled floors, slightly old-fashioned wooden furniture, built in 1970s and still under same family ownership. Great for families, beach toys for kids, kayaks, hobie cats, cots and highchairs, babysitting.

$$$$ Maca Bana Villas, Point Salines, T437-4395355, www.macabana.com. Perched on top of hill looking all along coastline to St George's, charming 1- to 2-bedroom villas, spacious and comfortable with state-of-the-art kitchen and open-plan living/dining area leading onto expansive veranda with hot tub and sunbeds, all solar powered, well designed and welcoming. Pretty gardens attract birds and butterflies while lizards clean up any unwanted insects. Walking distance from airport, where you can catch a bus. Activities organized including cookery class with chef from **Aquarium** restaurant below, painting class with owner/artist Rebecca on river bank, beach or waterfall, massages, reiki and spa treatments with visiting masseur. Short walk downhill to beach and restaurant, see Restaurants. They have their own organic farm to supply fruit and veg to guests and restaurant.

$$$$ Spice Island Beach Resort, Grand Anse, T473-4444423, www. spiceislandbeachresort.com. A luxury 5-star all-inclusive resort for couples and families. Cool white buildings with white roofs, warm colours for interior furnishings and bed covers. 64 very private and romantic suites of varying sizes, amazing bathrooms, on the beach with view to St George's and cruise ships, or in the garden with a sea view, all with flat screen TV, DVD player, double whirlpool bath, Italian linen and armfuls of bathroom goodies. Jamissa's spa for a range of treatments. Also an activity centre for children, the **Nutmeg Pod**, although children under 5 are not accepted in winter. Good food, own kitchen garden, self-sufficient in some organic veg.

$$$$ True Blue Bay Resort and Marina, True Blue Bay, T473-4438783, www.truebluebay.com. Small, intimate, helpful and friendly, British-Mexican owners, large rooms, suites, cottages and apartments, all colourfully painted, kitchenettes, a/c, fan, sea view, balconies with hammocks, child friendly, high chairs and play equipment, infinity pool with sandy shore and delightful fence of colourful pretend chattel houses around it, gym, spa/beauty treatments, car hire, dock facilities, boat charter available, dive shop on site, kayaks, hobie cats, **Dodgy Dock** restaurant and lounge bar over water, good food, Mexican specialities, also children's food and drink menu.

$$$$ Twelve Degrees North, Lance Aux Épines, T473-4444580, www. twelvedegreesnorth.com. Small complex of suites on the waterfront in lovely gardens with tennis, pool, sunfish, dock, kayaks, beach, snorkelling. Owner-managed by Joseph Gaylord, an excellent host, with an exceptional team of housekeepers who will shop and cook for you at no extra cost, providing delicious meals on your balcony. No children under 15.

$$$$-$$$ Allamanda Beach Resort, Grand Anse, T473-4440095, www. allamandaresort.com. 50 spacious rooms on 3 floors in blocks on narrow plot with beach access, rather dated style and some maintenance issues but good location right in the middle of Grand Anse, close to mall, bakery, cricket field, local lunch sellers and restaurants in walking distance. Service is friendly and helpful. Breakfast is included in most room rates but nothing special.

$$$$-$$$ Coral Cove Cottages, Lance aux Épines, T473-4444422, www.coralcovecottages.com. Opened 6 weeks before the Revolution, still under same ownership. Several, lovely, breezy, well-equipped self-catering cottages, 1 or 2 bedrooms, also apartments with larger kitchens, beautiful view of Atlantic coast, at the end of the road, 15 mins' walk to restaurants and minimarket, immaculate gardens, own beach and jetty with gazebo at the end, good snorkelling, shallow water, pool, tennis, very private and quiet, great for kids, attracts lots of repeat visitors, discounts for longer stays.

$$$$-$$$ Gem Holiday Beach Resort, Morne Rouge Bay, T473-4444224, www.gembeachresort.com. Rooms, suites with kitchen, a/c, balcony, good but not luxurious, comfortable living room with dining table, old but adequate kitchen units. Beach bar and restaurant **Sur la Mer** on beach, reasonable food, internet room, pool room, roof terrace for quiz nights and other activities, popular with guests, medical students and locals on Thu nights, also **Fantazia** night club attached.

$$$$-$$$ Jenny's Place, Silver Sands, Grand Anse, T473-4395186, www.jennysplacegrenada.com. At the northern, uncrowded end of the beach with **The Edge** restaurant on waterfront, 6 studios and suites and 1 budget room, sleep 2-4, huge rooms, ground floor wheelchair accessible, high ceilings, big bathrooms with bathtub and shower over, balcony, TV, a/c, fans, excellent value for location, comfortable, laid-back and interesting fellow guests. Friendly hosts are happy to arrange water taxis, water sports, tours and other activities. Get the bus into town, walk along the beach for other restaurants, everything is handy and convenient.

$$$$-$$$ Kalinago Beach Resort, Morne Rouge Bay, T473-4445255, www.kalinagobeachresort.com. Sister property and next to **Gem** on the beach, newer and more upmarket but still relaxed and peaceful, 29 suites with only the pool between them and the sea. Good restaurant in separate building with balcony serving mix of international and West Indian food.

$$$$-$$$ Siesta, Grand Anse, T473-4444646, www.siestahotel.com. Bright and white, functional, simple furnishings, no frills, friendly service. Variety of rooms, efficiencies, studios and 1- to 2-bedroom apartments with basic cooking facilities. Independent restaurant on site Wed-Mon 0700-1400. Not on beach and it's about 10-15 mins walk across busy roads to Grand Anse.

$$$ La Heliconia, on main road to airport, Point Salines, T473-4398585, www.laheliconia.com. Suites and apartments in walking distance of airport, Magazine Beach, Dr Groom's Beach, close to the university and on bus route into St George's. Spa and restaurant on site, both good. Pleasant staff and helpful hosts. Simple accommodation but if you have any problems they are soon sorted out.

Northern Grenada p42, map p27
$$$$ Petite Anse, T473-4425252, www.petiteanse.com. At the northern tip of the island on a secluded beach hemmed in by hills. Good base for exploring the north, including Levera, Bathway beach and the Carib jump at Sauteurs and turtle watching in season can be arranged. English owners Phillip and Annie Clift are on hand for any requests or information. A delightful and relaxing place to stay, chalet rooms all have sea view and some are only steps from the ocean with deck or terrace. Good restaurant using ingredients from the kitchen garden or locally sourced, mostly European or West Indian dishes, full English breakfast, even an espresso machine with proper coffee.

$$$ Almost Paradise, Sauteurs, T473-4420608, www.almost-paradise-grenada.com. Simple, breezy wooden rooms and cottages of varying sizes in delightful hillside garden setting with an amazing view to the Grenadines and the nicest place to stay this end of the island. Peaceful and relaxing, but if you want to get out and about there is lots to do close by. Outdoor shower, balconies with hammocks, kitchen corner in living room, colourful bedrooms, high ceilings, fans, solar power, small dark sand beach at bottom of hill, links with local boatmen for tours to Sandy Island, massages. Restaurant, see below, breakfast and dinner for guests, special diets can be catered for on request.

$$ Crayfish Bay Organic Estate, Non Pareil, T473-4421897, www.crayfishbay.com. A simple wooden cabin with 2 bedrooms and a loft area suitable for children on a working cocoa estate where fruit and vegetables are also grown and available for guests. Off the beaten track, you experience rustic village life. Self-catering, but breakfast with home-made bread and evening meal can be provided on request, often eaten with your hosts, family-style. Rum shops and buses in walking distance but restaurants are a drive away. Fans and mosquito nets provided but bring insect repellent. Guests are welcome to help on the farm or make cocoa tea balls after the harvest.

East coast Grenada *p42, map p27*
$$$$ La Sagesse, T473-4446458, www.lasagesse.com (see page 37).

Former residence of the late Lord Brownlow, a cousin of the Queen, the current owners have been here since 1987. Marvellous location, although room design leaves something to be desired. 12 rooms, some of which are in the 'manor house' and others built alongside beside the water although not all can see the sea. Beautiful setting on a sandy bay lined with coconut palms and cliffs at one end and a stream running into the sea. Service is special here and all the staff are friendly, use your name and make you feel like family. Open-air restaurant and beach bar, children friendly, also good for singles or romantic couples. Hiking trails over headland to neighbouring beaches for snorkelling. Buses to St George's pass the end of the road.

$$$$-$$$ Petit Bacaye Cottage Hotel, on bay of same name, Westerhall, T473-4432902, www.petitbacaye.com. Very desirable and relaxing place to stay, romantic hideaway on beach. 5 thatched cottages of different sizes, sleep 2, 40 m from the water with lovely sea views, no TV or radio, rates include tax and service, airport pick-up, welcome supplies. Bring your own beach towels and a torch. Colourful restaurant on the lawn by the beach for breakfast, lunch and dinner, or eat in the 'treehouse', mostly seafood, fishermen call daily with fish and lobster, reef and own bird sanctuary islet (egret roost) 200 m offshore in shallow water (bring water shoes), jeep and guide hire arranged, another sandy beach round the bluff.

$$$-$$ Grenada Rainbow Inn, Grenville, St Andrew's, T4427714, see facebook. Run by Neitha Williams (Aunty Nits) and her daughter Yvonne Williams, 15 rooms or apartments with kitchenette (sleep 4), with or without a/c, rooms vary, no smoking in rooms, some have small balcony, good local food served family style, good for groups, volunteers, charity workers, or people who want to experience village life, credit cards accepted.

$$ Sam's Inn, Dunfermline, T473-4427853, www.samsinn.com. 10 rooms with double and single bed, a/c or fans, and 3 2-bedroom apartments in modern block, some with TV, good-sized bathrooms have wardrobe in them, large balcony overlooking road, no smoking, restaurant and bar, country setting, view of Pearls Airport, small store close by. The late Mrs Ellen Sam opened the hotel in the 1970s when Pearls' limited flights meant passengers often needed to stay over. Nowadays the hotel is run by her son, daughter and son-in-law.

Carriacou *p50, map p51*

There are also rental villas and apartments on the island, try www.islandvillas.com, www.simplycarriacou.com or www.homeaway.co.uk.

$$$$-$$$ Bayaleau Point Cottages, Windward, T473-4437984, www.carriacoucottages.com. 4 lovely, well-equipped and colourful wooden cottages in chattel house style with verandas, hammocks, clean, own little beach, good snorkelling, owners Ulla and Dave Goldhill are helpful, friendly, dinner available several nights a week, good for children, lots of Labrador dogs, Wi-Fi. Simple, laid-back, island lifestyle. Dave's team will take you on his boat, *Mostly Harmless* to the Tobago Cays and other Grenadine islands for a wonderful day trip, swimming with turtles, snorkelling, lobster lunch on a beach, reggae rum punch on an island with nothing but a bar.

$$$$-$$$ Green Roof Inn, on hillside overlooking sea, 10 mins north of Hillsborough, just past the desalination plant, T473-4436399, www.greenroofinn.com. Swedish owned, 4 double rooms and 2 cottages in the garden, 1 with kitchenette, extra beds available, breakfast included, mosquito nets, fans, airport/jetty transfers, sandy area in front of hotel for swimming, day trips arranged. Tue-Sun for dinner, lunch on request, special diets catered for. Restaurant has spectacular views, roof, but no walls, mainly seafood, lobster, barracuda, swordfish, Caribbean ingredients, European preparation. Professional service and friendly staff.

$$$$-$$$ Laurena, Middle St, Hillsborough, T473-4438759, www.hotellaurena.com. Modern, central location, a/c rooms, suites and apartments, some with kitchenettes, with 2 rooms for the handicapped, good Wi-Fi, conference rooms. This is the largest hotel on the island but it suffers from maintenance and service issues. They sometimes run out of food for breakfast at the hotel. Its restaurant is in town, a short walk away.

$$$ Bogles Round House, Bogles, T473-4437841, www.boglesround house.com. 3 cottages, one with a/c, self-contained, sleep 2-4, comfortable, located away from the main tourist areas, path down to sea, kayaks available. Run by Roxanne and Phil, a British couple. Restaurant and bar serving local and European food and drinks daily except Wed, excellent breakfast, gourmet dinner. Reservations needed in low season or for large groups.

$$$ Carriacou Grand View, Belair Rd, overlooking Hillsborough, T473-4436348, www.carriacougrandview. com. Rooms and self-catering apartments high up on the hill, breezy, fans, a/c, TV, restaurant, bar, pool, good views, particularly from rooms on upper floors. High standard of service, Shirley and Earl are helpful and friendly, they know what is going on and where to go. Easy walk downhill to town, taxi US$6.50 back uphill with shopping.

$$$ Peace Haven Guesthouse, south of pier on seafront, Main St, Hillsborough, T473-4437475. Rooms on 1st floor large, each with kitchenette, fridge, fan, contact Lucille Atkins.

$$$-$$ Ade's Dream, T473-4437317, www.adesdream.com, Main St, Hillsborough. Economy rooms in annex share communal kitchen or studios in main building with own kitchenette, close to dock, well equipped, clean and popular, supermarket downstairs open daily, restaurant across the road with sea frontage.

$$$-$$ Millies Guesthouse, Main St, Hillsborough, T473-4436455, millies@ spiceisle.com. Room or 1-, 2- or 3-bedroomed apartments with kitchen, bathroom/shower, fans, a/c, ocean view, simple but clean and quiet.

Petite Martinique *p55*
$$ Melodie's Guesthouse, T473-4439052. 10 rooms, some with balconies, ceiling fans, shared kitchen, on the seafront, tours and water sports offered. In need of repairs and service poor, but there is little choice here and it's cheap, unlike Petit St Vincent across the water.

🍴 Restaurants

St George's *p28, map p29*
$$$ BB's Crabback Caribbean Restaurant, Progress House, at the end of the Carenage, T473-4357058, www.bbscrabback.com. Mon-Sat breakfast, lunch and dinner. Overlooking the water, lovely view of the harbour, friendly and welcoming with great food and drinks. Visitors have expressed their appreciation by writing on the walls. Local seafood dishes and meat specialities such as curry mutton, all tasty and beautifully presented. Owned by Brian Benjamin, who has a restaurant of the same name in west London.

$$$ Patrick's, Lagoon Rd, opposite Port Louis Marina, T473-4497234, see facebook. Mon-Sat 1100-2200, Sun 1830 until last guest leaves. Reservations needed. Sadly Patrick Levine died in 2010 but Karen Hall continues as chef and owner at this one-of-a-kind restaurant where the atmosphere is friendly and sociable and groups are encouraged. Fixed price dinner of up to 20 different dishes served tapas style and dessert. A huge variety and interesting combinations of local foods, breadfruit salad and green papaya salad are outstanding while you can also be offered stir fry rabbit, green papaya in cheese sauce, cou-cou, tannia cakes with shrimps, oildown with coconut cream, many dishes you may never have tried before. Everything will be explained to you. Cash or TCs only.

$$ Nutmeg, on the Carenage above the **Sea Change Book Store**, T473-4359525, see facebook. Mon-Sat 0800-2300, Sun 1600-2300. Under new ownership but still good for local dishes snacks, lunch, sandwiches, rotis, soups, salads or just a cold beer, get a table by the wide open windows overlooking the Carenage and the boats in the harbour.

$$-$ Creole Shack, Melville St overlooking cruise ships, T473-9376. Sun-Thu 0700-2200, Fri, Sat 0700-2400. Local food cafeteria style with a bar, above **Andall & Assoc** supermarket and popular at lunchtime with long queues, specials such as curry lambie, stew oxtail and salt fish souse, oildown and fresh juices. Karaoke Wed, Sat, Sun from 1800. Brunch on Sun.

$$-$ Deyna's Tasty Foods, Melville St, opposite waterfront bus station, T473-4406795. Mon-Sat 0800-2100, Sun 1000-1600. Good local food at local prices, and lots of it, breakfast will set you up for the day, rotis any time, crowded at lunch, separate queue for takeaway meals. Also good place to stop for a drink as a break from shopping or sightseeing, try sorrel, mauby or passionfruit.

Southwest Grenada *p35, map p27*

$$$ Aquarium Restaurant & La Sirena Beach Bar, Point Salines Beach, T473-4441410, www.aquarium-grenada.com. Tue-Sun 1000-late, dinner reservations requested. Wed specials, Sun barbeque with coal pit, showers, toilets, snorkelling offshore, great location, good food, lobster, fish, steak, sandwiches, live music and buffet from 1900 1st Sat in month, happy hour at La Sirena Fri. Very popular, particularly at weekends with families on the beach, same ownership as **Maca Bana Villas**, see page 57.

$$$ Beach House, Portici Beach, T473-4444455, www.beachhouse grenada.com. Mon-Sat lunch Dec-Mar 1130-1730, dinner all year 1800-2230, reservations preferred, can get water taxi from Carenage or shuttle service from hotels in south. Very pretty, open air, in gardens on the beach, hammocks, white cotton tablecloths and pillow cases for chairs. Good food, lots of oriental influences with sushi and satay, fish, steak and other meats, also good kids menu and yummy desserts.

$$$ Boots Cuisine, Grand Anse Valley Rd, Woodlands, T473-4442151, ruby_boots@hotmail.com. Mon-Sat 1100-1400, 1830-2200. Reservations required. Ruby and Roland (Boots) McSween run this small, delightful family restaurant serving excellent local food, a 5-course set meal with a choice of 3 mains, including melt-in-the-mouth lambi, delicious callaloo, goat, curried chicken, stew rabbit, grill fish, lobster, baked provisions and stew peas, must leave room for carambola pie and banana ice cream or bread pudding with nutmeg ice cream. Coming from Grand Anse Valley on Woodlands Rd, it is just before Clarkes Court on the right, small sign, rustic, open air dining under a roof, surrounded by plants. They will pick you up and return you to your lodging if you prefer, for EC$50.

$$$ Rhodes Restaurant, Calabash Hotel, T473-4444334. Open 1900-2130. Gary Rhodes' 1st restaurant outside the UK (now 2 more in Dubai) but always supervised by one of his top chefs to ensure consistent quality, using Rhodes' recipes and local ingredients. Open-air dining, daily specials, entertainment most nights, complimentary transport available.

$$$-$$ Coconut Beach, Grand Anse, T473-4444644, www. coconutbeachgrenada.com. Open 1230-2230, closed Tue. North of vendor's market, easy walk along the beach from the hotels. French Creole restaurant, jalousie windows opened to let in the breeze, colourful, painted purple, green, orange, picnic tables on beach so you can dine with your feet in the sand or more formal seating indoors, candlelit at night. Lots of fish and seafood, plenty of lobster, also steak, chicken and vegetarian dishes. Lunch time options of sandwiches, crêpes, omelettes, salads, local desserts such as coconut pie or opt for crêpes au chocolat.

$$$-$$ The Edge, at Jenny's Place, Silver Sands, Grand Anse, T473-4395186, see facebook. Open 1100-2200, closed Tue. At very northern point of beach, seafront bistro right on the water gets its name from its location. Variety of food, soups, pasta, salad, burgers, sandwiches for lunch or chicken curry, steak au poivre, catch of the day, pork tenderloin and other dishes for supper, or just come for a sunset drink and a light bite. Accommodation, see above.

$$$-$$ Red Crab, Lance aux Épines, T4444424, crab@spiceisle.com. Open 1100-1400, 1800-2300, closed Sun. Indoor and outdoor dining, but by a busy main road so you're best inside. Excellent local seafood, lobsterfest on Sat with prior reservation, good steak dinner, also soups, salads, sandwiches, burgers and catch of the day for lunch, live music Mon, Fri in season, darts Wed nights. Close to university, busy with students, service can suffer when it's full.

$$-$ La Boulangerie, Le Marquis Mall complex above Grand Anse Beach, T473-4441131. Mon-Sat 0830-2130, Sun 0900-2130. Good for breakfast with croissants, Danish pastries or full American, coffee and freshly squeezed juice, lunch and dinner of pizza and pasta, salads, sandwiches, Italian ice cream. Useful on a Sun night when most places are closed, they do takeaway meals too.

$$-$ Rumours, True Blue, by the university, T473-2314988, see facebook. Daily 1200-1400, closed Jul. A takeaway hut with outdoor seating in a group of similar places to catch the student trade. Vegetarian and vegan dishes and seafood, all cooked to order so fairly slow service, good veggie roti or pitta bread with curried chickpeas and tofu, all tasty and fresh.

Northern Grenada *p42, map p27*

$$$ Petite Anse, T473-4425252, www.petiteanse.com. At the northern tip of the island, the hotel restaurant looks out across the sea to the Grenadines. Home-grown or locally grown fruit and veg with a European take on West Indian dishes. Good coffee after the meal.

$$$-$$ Almost Paradise, Sauteurs, T473-4420608, www.almost-paradise-grenada.com. Tue-Sun 1200-1700, dinner by reservation only. Lovely location on hillside overlooking the Grenadines, run by Kate (Canadian) and Uwe (German) Baumann, who use all the local produce and make their own rum liqueurs as *digestifs*. Great place for a lunch stop in an island tour, fish, shrimp, soup, salads, home made bread and cocktails.

East coast Grenada *p42, map p27*

$$$-$$ La Sagesse (see page 37), T473-4446458 for reservations which are recommended, especially for dinner. Breakfast, lunch and dinner. Fresh lobster, grilled tuna, outdoor restaurant, beautiful location, walk it off afterwards, good hiking over the mountain, can provide return transport, lunch, guided nature walk with exotic fruit tasting, dinner packages available.

Carriacou *p50, map p51*

The market near the pier in Hillsborough comes alive on Mon when the produce is brought in. 'Jack Iron' rum (180° proof) is a local hazard, it is so strong that ice sinks in it. It is distilled in Barbados but bottled in Carriacou; it is cheap and is liberally dispensed on all high days and holidays (fairly liberally on other days too). Some basic local bar/restaurants often run out of food quite early or close in the evenings, check if they will be open for dinner. Finding cheap meals can be difficult at weekends. Several small bars and restaurants in Tyrell Bay do takeaways and other services for visiting yachts. For hotel restaurants, see Where to stay, above.

$$$-$$ Moringa, Esplanade, Hillsborough, T473-4438300, http://jb1.moringacarriacou.com. Open 1200-1600, 1800-2200, closed Tue and Sun lunch. Jean-Baptiste (JB) used to run the **Lazy Turtle** in Tyrell Bay, but now has this delightful restaurant and crêperie in Hillsborough on the waterfront under trees which are prettily lit at night. Beautiful food, local ingredients including lionfish. Good range of menu items, from soup, upmarket sandwiches and burgers for lunch, sweet and savoury crêpes any time (goat's cheese and caramelized apple is tasty), and full meals for dinner, using a variety of influences whether it is local callaloo, a Moroccan tagine or Thai curry.

$$$-$$ Slipway, Tyrell Bay, T473-4436500, http://slipwayrestaurant carriacou.com. Tue-Sat 1130-1400, 1800-2100, Sun 1130-1400, closed Mon, and Thu May-Nov. Restaurant in a converted old boatyard on the water's edge, excellent food, very popular with locals and yachties, reservations needed evenings and Sun. Limited menu but everything is fresh, great tuna carpaccio if available, also good steak, mahi mahi and burgers. Let them know if you're a vegetarian when you make your reservation.

$$ Off the Hook Bar & Grill, Paradise Beach, L'Esterre. Rustic wooden beach bar offering fish and chips, lambi, pizza, cold beer. Wed night bonfire on the beach. Sometimes live music. The owner, Curtis, will take you in his boat out to Sandy Island.

$$-$ Gallery Café, Tyrell Bay, T473-4437069, see facebook. Open 0700-1600. Breakfast and lunch. Good breakfasts, a mid-morning snack of Italian coffee and home-made cake, tasty lunches, from a popular seafood salad to great toasted sandwiches. Everything prepared freshly and nicely presented. Part of an arts and crafts gallery, free Wi-Fi, sit indoors or on the veranda.

$$-$ Hardwood Bar, Paradise Beach, L'Esterre. Open for lunch and dinner, snacks, drinks, beach bar, menu includes catch of the day and other seafood, also chicken and roti. Snorkelling gear for rent, water taxi service to Sandy Island or other places.

$$-$ Kayak Kafe & Juice Bar, Main St, Hillsborough, T473-4062151. Breakfast 0730-1100, lunch until 1430. Pleasant seating on veranda overlooking the sea by the ferry dock, wooden tables and chairs a mix of pastel colours for a cool, calm atmosphere. Extensive menu from full English breakfast to lamb fritters, good-sized portions of filling food and delicious juices and smoothies.

$$-$ Lazy Turtle Pizzeria and Bar, Tyrell Bay, T473-4438322, VHF16,

www.lazyturtlewi.com. Mon-Sat 1100-2300. Pizzeria, also pasta, seafood and meat dishes, bar, free Wi-Fi, friendly staff, lovely view over Tyrell Bay, popular with the yachting crowd.

Petite Martinique *p55*
$$-$ Palm Beach Restaurant and Bar, T473-4439103, VHF 16, www. petitemartinique.com/restaurant. Mon-Sat 0800-2200, Sun 1400-2200. Seafood, ribs and chicken, free water taxi service for those anchored in Petit St Vincent.

🎵 Bars and clubs

Grenada *p26, map p27*
Bananas, True Blue Rd, T473-4444662, http://bananas.gd. Open from 1600 or 1700, until 0400 Fri, 0300 Sat, 0200 Tue, 0100 Wed, 2300 Thu, Sun, happy hour 1700-1900, closed Mon. Sports bar, pizzas, burgers and restaurant, club with party nights popular with university students. Events have different entries. See facebook for what's on.

The Deck, Le Phare Bleu, Petite Calivigny Bay, T473-4442400, www. lepharebleu.com. Sat night live music ranging from easy-listening to full on party bands with dancing. See facebook for what's on at the restaurant/bar. Wed is a good night for meeting people when food is served family-style and everyone sits round a big table. Owner Dieter Burkhalter also hosts dinghy concerts when sailors arrive in their dinghies (there's a barge for landlubbers) for live bands playing on the old tug boat, *Calico*.

Dodgy Dock, at True Blue Bay, T437-4438783, www.dodgydock.com, moorings available. Daily 0700-2300, happy hour 1700-1800. Built out over the water under tent roof, lovely design, great cocktails, live music Tue, Fri, Sat, tango and Latin dance class Thu 1900-2030, EC$30, with dancing after. Pleasant for sundowner or after dinner drink, popular Fri after work lime 1800 when drinks are at happy hour prices if you order a platter for 2.

Fantazia 2001 Cultural Centre, Gem Holiday Beach Resort, Morne Rouge Beach, T473-4442288, http://fantazia2001niteclub.com. Open 2400-dawn. Doesn't get going until after midnight, even midweek. Circular dance floor with seating along the sides, mixed clientele depending on the night, funky, soca, fast calypso, reggae, hot and steamy, best night is Wed when they have old soul and reggae – 'blast from the past', or 'oldie goldies', Fri ladies free before midnight, see facebook for what's on.

Gouave Fish Fry, Gouave. Fri night from 1900. Lots of stalls selling different seafood with a variety of recipes, shrimp kebabs, baked fish in garlic sauce, stir fry lobster with noodles, fried snapper, jack etc, grilled lobster. Walk around and look at everything before you make your choice. Popular, busy and crowded. Live entertainment at one end of the street, including drum music and folk dancing. Goes on quite late but the best food runs out so best to get there before 2130.

Grenada Yacht Club, St George's, T473-4403050, www.grenadayacht club.com. Sun, Mon 1000-2200, Tue-Thu, Sat 1000-2300, Fri 1000-0100. Yachtsmen and others welcome, great place to sit and watch the boats entering the lagoon (and see if they are paying attention to the channel markers or run aground).

Junction Bar & Grill, L'Anse aux Épines, T473-4201086, see facebook. Wed-Sat evenings only. Always something going on, DJ or live music, Latin nights or karaoke, always popular for a Fri night lime, a fun place with friendly staff, good service and food, burgers particularly good.

Prickly Bay Marina, Lance Aux Épines, T473-4395265, see facebook. Open-air bar and pizza place popular with ex-pats and yachties. Live music Fri with DJ and dancing afterwards, busy, popular, crowded. Wed bingo, Tue quiz night, Sun movies. Look out for special deals on beer or pizza.

⊕ Entertainment

Grenada *p26, map p27*
Cinemas
Movie Palace, Excel Plaza, Grand Anse, T473-4446688, www.moviepalace.gd.

Theatres
Marryshow Folk Theatre in the University of the West Indies building on Tyrell St. Has concerts, plays and special events.

Spice Basket Theatre, Beaulieu, St George's, T473-4379000, www.spicebasketgrenada.com, has occasional concerts and other performances. Every Tue at 1830 there is Heritage Night, a dinner show, starting with a museum tour, then rum and chocolate tasting, followed by a buffet dinner, steel pan music, a video, dance show and open dance floor until 2200, US$75 to include unlimited drinks and transport from and to local hotels. Fri night there is a dinner, DJ, live band and dancing. Outdoor seating can be a problem if it rains, but it's good fun.

○ Shopping

Grenada *p26, map p27*
Arts and crafts
Art and Soul Gallery, Spiceland Mall, Grand Anse, T437-4393450, http://artandsoulgrenada.com. Mon-Sat 1000-1800. Fine art gallery, showcasing the work of Susan Mains, Oliver Benoit, Asher Mains, Marie Messenger and others.
Grenada Craft Centre, Lagoon Rd, next to **Tropicana Inn**, St George's. Houses Grenadian craftspersons selling jewellery, pottery, batik, wood, basketry and T-shirts.
White Cane Industries, on the Carenage adjacent to the Ministry of Health. Features a wide variety of arts and crafts made by blind or partially sighted people.
The Yellow Poui Art Gallery, Young St, , St George's, T473-4403001. Mon-Fri 0900-1600, Sat 0915-1215. Sells Grenadian and other Caribbean paintings, sculpture, photography, antique prints and engravings.

Market
Farmers' Night Market, Grenada Rainbow Inn, Grenville, T442 62777. 1st Thu of every month except Sep.

Featuring farm produce, arts and crafts, wine, food, music and farm animals; a social event, good shopping and fun for children.
St George's Market is busiest on a Sat when farmers come in from out of town with huge quantities of colourful fruit and vegetables, sold on tables under umbrellas, but local products such as spices and cocoa balls, gift baskets and crafts can be found any weekday in the covered market. Ask permission before taking photos of people.

Shopping malls
Esplanade Mall, on the Esplanade by the cruise ship terminal. Duty-free shops, gift shops, juice bars, pizza and US fast food, internet café, tourist bureau, toilets, phones. Outside there are craft stalls but only a short walk away is the market for a more authentic experience.

Spice products
Grenada prides itself on its spices, which are ideal souvenirs and are cheaper in the supermarket than on the street or in the market, but perhaps not so prettily packaged.
Arawak Islands Ltd, Frequente Industrial Park, T473-4443577, www.arawak-islands.com. Factory and retail outlet, Mon-Fri 0830-1630. They make a range of spices, sauces, herbal teas, candied nutmeg pods, natural perfumes, soap, bath goodies and massage oils, scented candles and incense sticks; mail order available.
De la Grenade Industries, T473-4403241, www.delagrenade.com.

Makes nutmeg jams, jellies, syrups, sauces and drinks, available in supermarkets and groceries. Their nutmeg syrup is an essential ingredient for a Grenadian rum punch, also delicious on pancakes. Their shop and garden are open to the public, see page 34.

The Grenada Co-operative Nutmeg Association, Lagoon Rd, T473-4402117, gcnanutmeg@spiceisle.com. Purchases nutmeg from its membership of 7000 farmers and markets it worldwide. It sells nutmeg oil in 15 ml and 30 ml bottles. See page 41 for tours of the processing plant in Gouyave.

○ What to do

Grenada *p26, map p27*
Cricket

The island's main land sport is played from Jan-Jun. Informal cricket is played on any piece of flat ground or on the beaches, but international test matches are played at the **Queen's Park National Stadium**, north of St George's. Built in 1998, it became the 84th Test venue when the West Indies played New Zealand there in 2002, but it was destroyed by Hurricane Ivan in 2004. It was refurbished for the 2007 Cricket World Cup (6 Super-8 matches were played there) with the help of the Chinese, to give it a capacity of 13,000 seats. The stadium hosts cricket, football, athletics, cycling, cultural events and exhibitions, although the Chinese are now building a football and athletics stadium as well. There are also training and practice grounds around the island.

Cycling

Mocha Spoke, True Blue, just off the road going to the university, T473-5332470, http://mochaspoke.com. Not only a bike rental place but also a cafe serving good coffee, proper espresso, cold drinks and smoothies. They have a good range of mountain bikes and tourers for men and women, can offer lots of advice on the best routes or take you on a guided tour. Bike rental US$20 per day, US$100 per week. 2½-hr south Grenada guided tour, US$49, 3½-hr Annandale Falls tour, US$59, including transfers to local hotels.

Diving

There is usually a dive company at any of the larger resorts. The nearest recompression chamber is in Barbados or Trinidad, both 30 mins by air ambulance. Members of the **Grenada Scuba Diving Association** all carry oxygen on board their boats.
Aquanauts Grenada, T473-4441126, www.aquanautsgrenada.com. Based at the **True Blue Bay Marina** with another branch at **Spice Island Beach Resort**, Grand Anse, offering a full range of courses and activities and easy access to a variety of dive sites. A 2-tank dive is US$110 including tank and weights, US$136 with all the gear, and a day trip with diving to Isle de Rhonde for advanced divers only, weather permitting, is US$143, tax included.
Dive Grenada, Flamboyant Hotel, T4441092, www.divegrenada.com. A PADI 5-star and BSAC operation, PADI courses (Open Water US$550), wreck dives for experienced divers,

Diving and snorkelling around Grenada and Carriacou

The reefs around Grenada provide excellent sites for diving. A popular dive is to the wreck of the Italian cruise liner, *Bianca C*. Other dive sites include **Boss Reef, The Hole, Valley of Whales, Forests of Dean, Grand Mal Point** (wall dive), **Dragon Bay** (wall dive) ends at Molinière, **Happy Valley** (drift with current to Dragon Bay). Three wrecks from cargo ships off Quarantine Point, St George's, are in strong currents. **Molinière** reef for beginners to advanced has a sunken sailboat, the *Buccaneer*; **Whibble** reef is a slopey sand wall (advanced drift dive); **Channel** reef is a shallow reef at the entrance to St George's with many rusted ships' anchors; **Spice Island** reef is for resort dives and beginners as well as the wrecks *Red Buoy*, *Veronica L* and *Quarter Wreck*. Dive sites around Carriacou include **Kick Em Jenny** (a submarine volcano), **Isle de Rhonde, Sandy Island, Sister Rocks** (to 100 ft, strong currents), **Twin Sisters** (walls to 180 ft and strong currents), **Mabouya Island,** **Saline Island** (drift dive). Local dive shops and agencies are working towards setting up a marine park to preserve the underwater world of Carriacou. The reefs are unspoilt, with forests of soft corals growing up to 10 ft tall with a wide range of creatures living among them. Dive sites are reached with a 10-15 minute boat ride and the reefs are about 20- to 30-ft down. There is no shore diving. In 2005 a 1960s tugboat, Westsider, was sunk as a wreck dive site in the planned marine park and has already been colonized by marine life.

The best **snorkelling** is around Molinière Point and up to Dragon Bay and Flamingo Bay. Flamingo Bay is named after a snail, not a bird. Snorkelling trips by boat will usually bring you to this area, often in the afternoons so that divers on board can do a shallow dive as well. You can see a wide variety of fish and invertebrates on the rocks and coral, even moray eels in holes if you look carefully.

---

night dives (US$75), snorkelling (US$48). A 2-tank dive is US$120, while a package of 6 dives is US$320. Equipment rental US$15 per dive.

Fishing

Deep-sea fishing can be arranged through **True Blue Sportfishing**, Port Louis Marina, T473-4074688, www.yesaye.com, with Captain Gary Clifford, and **Wayward Wind Fishing Charters**, T473-5389821, www.grenadafishing.com, with Captain Stewart. At the end of Jan each year, Grenada hosts **the Spice Island Billfish Tournament**, www.sibtgrenada.com, T473-4353842 for information, or see facebook.

Golf

Grenada Golf and Country Club, Woodlands, above Grand Anse, T473-4444128. Daily 0800 to sunset, but

Grenada Underwater Sculpture Park

Molinière Bay is the site of the most unusual dive and snorkel site, being the resting place for a growing collection of sculptures which are fast becoming an artificial reef. The bay, just north of St George's, is now a marine protected area. The first statues were carved out of concrete in 2006 by Jason deCaires Taylor, who has been a prolific contributor to the park, followed by Troy Lewis, a Grenadian potter. There are Amerindian cultural influences to some of the works, together with the humorous sponsored cyclist and the iconic Christ of the Deep statue, which commemorated 50 years since the *Bianca C* caught fire and sank. See http://grenadaunderwatersculpture.com.

only till 1200 on Sun. A 9-hole golf course with 18 tee boxes. A round of 9 holes with club hire, balls and caddy is US$55.

Kayaking
Conservation Kayak, Whisper Cove Marina, Lower Woburn, T473-4495248, www.conservationkayak.com. Tuition and tours around Woburn Bay and out to Hog Island, to wetlands and mangroves to see birds and other wildlife, fishing villages, a variety of routes, US$70-115, including use of waterproof cameras.

Sailing
Sailing in the waters around Grenada and through the Grenadines, via Carriacou, is very good. Bareboat or skippered charters and learn-to-sail holidays are all available, see http://grenadagrenadines.com/explore/yachting/charters/. There are also lots of companies offering day sails, no shortage of choice, many of them catering for the cruise ship market.

Carib Cats, T473-4443222, www.travelgrenadagrenadines.com/sailing.html. Full-day sailing, snorkelling, sunset, moonlight or party cruises on a 60-ft catamaran or 40-ft trimaran.
First Impressions, T473-4403678 (Mosden Cumberbatch), www.catamaranchartering.com. Catamarans for all types of charters, day, sunset, 14 different tours offered including whale watching.

Tennis
Hotels have courts and public courts are found at Grand Anse and Tanteen, St George's.

Tour operators
Lots of companies offer day tours of the island, stopping to visit waterfalls, nutmeg processing plants, and have lunch in the north or a picnic on Bathway beach. These are usually in minibuses or small buses and are primarily designed to give cruise ship passengers a taste of the island, so they can seem rushed.

Whale watching

Humpback whales can be seen off Grenada and Carriacou during their migrations in December-April. Pilot whales, dolphins and several other whales are also found in Grenadian waters.

Contact Mosden Cumberbatch (see Sailing, above) for whale-watching tours, he has a boat especially designed for whale watching, taking up to 35 people on a four-hour trip.

Ecotrek (part of **Ecodive** at the Coyaba Beach Resort and at Port Louis Marina), T437-4447777, www.ecodiveandtrek.com. They offer something a bit different including coastal, rainforest and mountain walks and island safaris, tailor-made tours for small groups or even a single person.

Henry's Safari Tours, T473-4445313, VHF channel 68, www.henrysafari.com. Dennis Henry conducts tours of the island and is very well informed on all aspects of Grenada. Henry's also services yachts, dealing with laundry, gas, shopping, etc. If there is anything you want to do, he'll arrange it somehow.

Mandoo Tours, T473-4401428, www.grenadatours.com. Island tours and trekking, Concord Falls, Mt Qua Qua, Seven Sisters Falls, lots of options.

Telfer Hiking Tours, Telfer Bedeau in the village of Soubise on the east coast offers guided hikes; you must ask around for him (or leave a message on T473-4426200 or see if the Tourism Department can put you in touch). Hikes to the Seven Falls, Mt Qua Qua, Claboney, Hot Springs, Concord Falls, about US$80 for a half-day hike for 2 people.

Water sports

Windsurfing, waterskiing and parasailing all take place off Grand Anse beach. Inshore sailing on sunfish, sailfish and hobiecats is offered by Grand Anse and Lance aux Épines hotels and operators.

Adventure Tours Grenada, T437-4445337, www.adventuregrenada.com. Offer tubing on the Balthazar river, a mild, 1½-hr adventure suitable for ages 8 years and up, US$45. They also offer jeep tours of the island and bicycle rental.

Carriacou *p50, map p51*
Diving

Arawak Divers, Tyrell Bay, T473-4436906, www.arawakdivers.com. They use two boats, a Boston whaler and a pirogue, with a boat captain on board at all times. A 2-tank dive costs US$99 including tank and weights. Equipment rental is US$15 per dive. Also single (US$35 half day, US$55 whole day) and tandem (US$45/US$70) kayak rentals.

Deefer Diving at Main St, Hillsborough, T473-4437882, www.deeferdiving.com. Run by Alex and Gary Ward, this PADI 5-star operation uses a custom-built catamaran, taking

Boat information

Ports of entry: (own flag) St George's, Prickly Bay, St David's Harbour and Grenville on Grenada, Hillsborough and Tyrell Bay on Carriacou. Prickly Bay (Lance Aux Épines) and St David's are for yachts only. The Grenada Ports Authority (www.grenadaports.com) has full details of port fees, anchorages and marinas. Marinas cater for all sizes of craft, from small to mega-yachts; many marinas are expanding their capacity and new facilities are being developed. Blue Lagoon Marina is in St George's Bay, Clarkes Court Marina is in Woburn Bay, Grenada Marine is in St David's Harbour (full-service boatyard with haul-out facility and six acres of storage), Grenada Yacht Club is in the Lagoon in St George's, Martin's Marina is at Lance aux Épines, Spice Island Marine Services is in Prickly Bay, Prickly Bay Marina is also here, True Blue Bay Marina is near to Prickly Bay, Le Phare Bleu Marina & Resort is in Petite Calivigny Bay. On Carriacou, a new, full-service marina is being built at Tyrell Bay, where Tyrell Bay Haulout already provides haul-out services and storage.

small groups with a flexible itinerary. Partners and families can snorkel for free while you dive. A 2-tank dive is US$104.50 including tank and weights. US$2 reef tax per person per day goes towards maintaining the marine protected area.

Tour operators

Taxi drivers will offer to take you on a tour of the island, the tourist office will give you a recommendation or else contact the **Carriacou Owners and Drivers Association**, T473-4437386, VHF16. A full tour of the island is set at US$50 for 2½ hrs. Several captains offer tours of nearby islands by boat. Be sure to check safety equipment, they are not licensed. If the engine fails has he got oars or sails as an alternative? Is there a radio? Life jackets? A motor boat on its way to White Island for a picnic broke down and drifted for 3 days, eventually being found off the Venezuelan coast. **Water taxis** will also take you on trips to the little islands offshore or to other Grenadines close by. The Tobago Cays are a popular day trip.

⊖ Transport

Grenada p26, map p27
Air
See pages 6 and 28 for flights to the islands and airport information.

Boat
See page 11 for how to get there by sea and box, above, for boat information.

Bus

Buses or minivans (look for the letter H on the number plate) run to all parts of the island from the bus station on the Esplanade in St George's. Fares are EC$2.50 for any journey starting and finishing within the same parish and for any journey of 3 miles or less, eg St George's to Grand Anse. See page 35, for further information.

Car

Cars can be rented from a number of companies for about US$65-75 a day (cheaper for longer), plus US$2,500 excess liability and 5% tax (payable by credit card). The tourist office has a list of car hire agencies, see http:// www.grenadagrenadines.com/plan/ getting-around/rental-cars.

Taxi

Fares are set by the tourist board on a per mile basis. See page 12 for further details.

Carriacou *p50, map p51*
Air

See pages 6 and 50 for flight and airport details and how to get to Carriacou. Disconcertingly, the main road goes straight across the runway, traffic is halted when aircraft are due.

Boat

Osprey Lines, T473-4408126 (Grenada), T473-4438126 (Carriacou), www.ospreylines.com. A punctual and efficient hovercraft service continuing to Petite Martinique. Office in Hillsborough on the corner of Main St and Paterson St, get ticket in advance if you want to catch the early morning boat, then you can just walk straight on with your luggage. See pages 11 and 73 for other ferry services.

Bus

Buses go from Hillsborough to **Bogles**, **Windward** and to **Tyrell Bay**. To get from Tyrell Bay to Windward you would have to change buses in Hillsborough. The same van may be a taxi, ask for 'bus' and be prepared to wait. There are also plenty of taxis and water taxis.

❶ Directory

Grenada *p26, map p27*
Medical services St George's **General Hospital**, Fort George's Point, T473-4402050. There is also the private **St Augustine Medical Centre**, T473-4406173. **Black Rock Medical clinic**, Grand Anse Shopping Centre, has 24-hr emergency service. On Carriacou there is the **Princess Royal Hospital**, Belair, T473-4437400, Windward Health Clinic, T473-4436425, and **Hillsborough Health Clinic**, 2nd Av, T473-4439198. **Ambulance:** T434 in St George's, T724 in St Andrew's and T774 on Carriacou.

St Vincent

St Vincent is green and fertile with a lush rainforest and mountainous interior, beautiful volcanic beaches and fishing villages, coconut groves and banana plantations. Hiking and birdwatching are rewarding activities on this quiet island, which is relatively uncommercialized for tourism. Underwater, diving and snorkelling on the unspoiled reefs offer a colourful adventure with a huge array of sea creatures to identify.

St Vincent is widely known for the superb sailing conditions provided by its 32 sister islands and cays and most visitors spend some time on a yacht, even if only for a day. Bareboat and crewed yachts are available for wherever you want to go. There are also very competitive regattas and yacht races held throughout the year, accompanied by a lot of parties and social events. Alternatively you can hop on a ferry or the mail boat and travel as Vincentians do. Accommodation is low key in small hotels and guesthouses; there are no all-inclusive resorts dominating the beaches of this island.

Arriving in St Vincent

Getting there There are no direct flights from Europe or North America but same-day connecting flights are available through Barbados, Grenada, St Lucia, Martinique, Puerto Rico and Trinidad. This should change when the new Argyle International Airport is completed with a longer runway for long haul aircraft. You can also get charter flights on small planes from Barbados to St Vincent, Bequia, Mustique, Canouan and Union Island. Many people arrive on yachts, having sailed across the Atlantic or through the Caribbean. There is an informal international ferry on a small local boat between Union Island and Carriacou (Grenada). ⏵ *See Transport, pages 11 and 98, for further details.*

Getting around

Flights within the Grenadines are cheap and reliable. **SVG Air, Grenadine Air Alliance** and **Mustique Airways** fly daily scheduled services from St Vincent to Bequia, Mustique, Canouan and Union Island. There are several ferries and a mail boat between St Vincent, Bequia, Canouan, Mayreau and Union Island. Most, but not all, of the islands have a cheap bus service, which can be a minibus or a pick-up truck with seats in the back. Car hire is available on St Vincent and Bequia.

Kingstown → *For listings, see pages 90-99.*

The capital, Kingstown, stands on a sheltered bay and is surrounded on all sides by steep, green hills, with houses perched all the way up. However, it is a generally unattractive port city with the waterfront dominated by the container port, cruise ship terminal, fish market and bus station. There is no promenade along the seafront and buildings along the reclaimed land look inland rather than out to sea. Nevertheless, an active beautification association is making huge strides in cleaning up the city, with overgrown bridges repaired or rebuilt, buildings painted and re-roofed and plants maintained. Some buildings have been demolished. The most attractive and historical buildings are inland along the three main parallel streets: **Bay Street**, **Long Lane** and **Grenville/Halifax Street**, also known as Front Street, Middle Street and Back Street.

Places in Kingstown

Kingstown is known as the 'city of arcades' and it is possible to walk around most of the centre under cover. There are even building regulations to encourage the practice in new construction. The shopping and business area is no more than two blocks wide, running between Bay Street and Halifax Street/ Grenville Street. The **New Kingstown Fish Market**, built with Japanese aid, was opened in 1990 near the Police Headquarters. This complex, known as **Little**

St Vincent

Caribbean Sea

Baleine Bay
Commantawana Bay
Salt Pond
Fancy
Owia
Owia Bay
Falls of Baleine
Sandy Bay
Waterloo Mountains
Sandy Bay
Larikai Bay
La Soufrière (4173 ft)
Overland Village
Wallibou Beach
Orange Hill
Wallibou
Petit Wallibou
Rabacca Dry River
CHATEAUBELAIR ISLAND
Richmond
Dark View Falls
Morne Garu Mountains
Georgetown
Rose Bank
Chateaubelair
Richmond Peak (3523 ft)
Mt Brisbane (3058 ft)
Troumaka Bay
Troumaka
Coulis Hill
Rose Hall
Chester Cottage
Cumberland Bay
Cumberland
Black Point
Coco
Spring Village
Byera Beach
Wallilabou Bay
Grove
South Rivers
Friendly
Hermitage
Barrouallie
Colonarie Basin
Sans Souci
Colonarie Bay
Mt Wynne Bay
Petroglyphs
Vermont Nature Trail
North Union
Buccament Valley
Montreal Gardens
Greiggs
Layou
Vermont
Biabou
Grant's Bay
Buccament Bay
Peniston
Mount St Andrew (2413 ft)
Camel
Questelles
Mesopotamia
Peruvian Vale
Anse Cayenne
Camden Park
Botanical Gardens
Evesham
Yambou River
Lowmans Bay
Fort Charlotte
Belmont
Petroglyph
Argyle Beach
Johnson Pt
Kingstown
Escape Estate
Yambou Head
Rawacou
Mt Pleasant Beach
Kings Hill Forest Reserve
Stubbs
Kingstown Bay
Arnos Vale
Stubbs Bay
Cane Garden Point
Villa
Brighton Village
Indian Bay
Calliaqua
Brighton Beach
Milligan Cay
YOUNG ISLAND
Fort Duvernette
Sharp's Bay

N

3 km
3 miles

Where to stay 🛏

Beachcombers **1**
Buccament Bay **2**
Grand View Beach **1**
Mariners **1**
Paradise Beach **1**
Sea Breeze Guest House **8**
Sunset Shores **1**
Tranquility Beach **9**
Villa Lodge **1**
Young Island Resort **11**

Expulsion of the Garifuna

By the time Columbus discovered St Vincent on his third voyage in 1498, the Kalinago (Caribs) were occupying the island, which they called Hairoun. They had overpowered the Arawak-speaking people, who had arrived and settled there a few centuries earlier, killing the men but interbreeding with the women. The Kalinago aggressively prevented European settlement until the 18th century but were more welcoming to Africans. In 1675 a passing Dutch ship laden with settlers and their slaves was shipwrecked between St Vincent and Bequia. Only the slaves survived and these settled and mixed with the native population and their descendants still live in Sandy Bay and a few places in the northwest. Escaped slaves from St Lucia and Grenada later also sought refuge on St Vincent and interbred with the Kalinago. As they multiplied they became known as 'Black Caribs' or Garifuna. There was tension between the Kalinago and the Black Caribs and in 1700 there was civil war.

In 1722 the British attempted to colonize St Vincent but French settlers had already arrived and were living peaceably with the Kalinago growing tobacco, indigo, cotton and sugar. Possession was hotly disputed until 1763 when it was ceded to Britain. It was lost to the French again in 1778 but regained under the Treaty of Versailles in 1783. However, this did not bring peace with the Black Caribs, who repeatedly tried to oust the British in what became known as the Carib Wars. A treaty with them in 1773 was soon violated by both sides. Peace came only at the end of the century when in 1796 General Abercrombie crushed a revolt fomented the previous year by the French radical Victor Hugues. In 1797, over 5000 Black Caribs were deported to Roatán, an island at that time in British hands off the coast of Honduras. The violence ceased although racial tension took much longer to eradicate. In the late 19th century, a St Vincentian poet, Horatio Nelson Huggins wrote an epic poem about the 1795 Carib revolt and deportation to Roatán, called Hiroona, which was published in the 1930s.

Slavery was abolished in 1832 but social and economic conditions remained harsh for the majority non-white population. In the 19th century labour shortages on the plantations brought Portuguese immigrants in the 1840s and East Indians in the 1860s. The population today is largely a mixture of these, the African slaves and the Black Caribs.

Tokyo, has car parking and is the point of departure for minibuses to all parts of the island. On Halifax Street at the junction with South River Road is the Old Public Library, an old stone building with a pillared portico. Also known as the **Carnegie Building**, its construction was paid for by the US philanthropist, Andrew Carnegie, and the library opened in 1909. In the late 20th century the library moved into a newer, larger building and was replaced by the Alliance

Kingstown

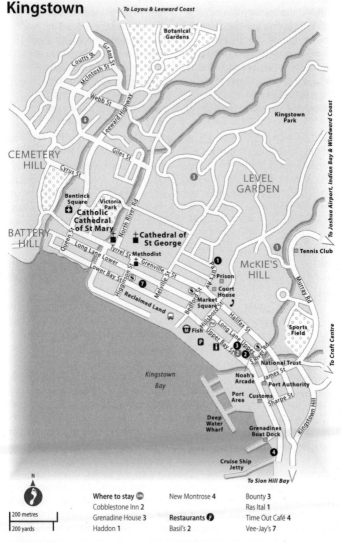

Where to stay 🛏	New Montrose 4	Bounty 3
Cobblestone Inn 2		Ras Ital 1
Grenadine House 3	Restaurants 🍴	Time Out Café 4
Haddon 1	Basil's 2	Vee-Jay's 7

Government in St Vincent and the Grenadines

In 1925 a Legislative Council was inaugurated but universal adult suffrage was not introduced until 1951. St Vincent and the Grenadines belonged to the Windward Islands Federation until 1959 and the West Indies Federation between 1958 and 1962. In 1969 the country became a British Associated State with complete internal self-government. In 1979 St Vincent and the Grenadines gained full Independence. St Vincent and the Grenadines is a constitutional monarchy within the Commonwealth. The Queen is represented by a Governor General. There is a House of Assembly with 15 elected representatives and six senators.

Française, who made it their headquarters. They still occupy the first floor, but the ground floor is the home of the **National Trust of St Vincent and the Grenadines** and houses the **National Archaeological Collection** ① *T4512921, www.svgnationaltrust.org, Mon-Thu 0900-1700, Fri 0900-1600, EC$5/US$2.* Archaeological evidence shows that Saladoid Amerindians from the Orinoco region of South America arrived in St Vincent around AD160 and there was a large settlement in the Argyle area. They knew how to weave, work stone and carve canoes. Artefacts and decorative pottery illustrate how they lived and ran their society, what tools they used, what they ate and how they cooked their food, as well as what jewellery they wore. There are several petroglyphs around the island, such as at Layou, Buccament, Barrouallie, Petit Bordel and Chateaubelaire, and some on Canouan and Petit St Vincent.

The **Market Square** in front of the Court House is the hub of activity. A new covered market with cream and brown horizontal stripes has been built from Upper Bay to Halifax Street. Fruit and vegetables are downstairs and clothing is upstairs. In the middle of the market building is a circular area where farmers sell their produce on Fridays.

Kingstown has two cathedrals, St George's (Anglican) and St Mary's (Roman Catholic). **St George's**, consecrated in 1820, has an airy nave and a pale blue gallery running around the north, west and south sides. It became a cathedral in 1877 when the Diocese of the Windward Islands was constituted and the chancel and transepts date from 1880 to 1887. The cupula was blown down by a hurricane in 1898 and after that battlements were added to the tower. There is an interesting floor plaque in the nave, now covered by carpet, commemorating a general who died fighting the Caribs. Other interesting features include a memorial to Sir Charles Brisbane (1772-1829) who captured Curaçao. A lovely stained-glass window in the south transept was reputedly commissioned by Queen Victoria on the death of her grandson. She took exception to angels in red rather than the traditional white and it was put

Flora and fauna

St Vincent has a wide variety of tropical plants, most of which can be seen in the **Botanical Gardens**, where conservation of rare species has been practised since they were founded in 1765. There you can see the mangosteen fruit tree and one of the few examples of *Spachea perforata*, a tree once thought to be found only in St Vincent but now found in other parts of the world, as well as the famous third generation sucker of the original breadfruit tree brought by Captain Bligh of the *Bounty* in 1793 from Tahiti. Other conservation work taking place in the gardens involves the endangered St Vincent parrot, *Amazona guildingii*, which is the national bird. An aviary, originally containing birds confiscated from illegal captors, now holds 12 parrots. The main colonies are around Buccament, Cumberland-Wallilabou, Linley-Richmond and Locust Valley-Colonarie Valley. A parrot reserve is being established in the upper Buccament Valley.

Another protected bird unique to St Vincent is the whistling warbler, and this, as well as the black hawk, the cocoa thrush, the crested hummingbird, the red-capped green tanager, green heron and other species can be seen, or at least heard, in the Buccament Valley. There are nature trails starting near the top of the valley, passing through tropical forest, and it is possible to picnic. The Forestry Department have prepared official trail plans. A pamphlet details the Vermont Nature Trails, Wallilabou Falls, Richmond Beach, Owia Salt Pond and La Soufrière Volcano Trails.

into storage in St Paul's Cathedral. It was brought to St Vincent in the 1930s. **St Mary's** is of far less sober construction, with different styles, Flemish, Moorish, Byzantine and Romanesque, all in dark grey stone, crowded together on the church, presbytery and school. Building went on throughout the 19th century, with renovation in the 1940s. The exterior of the church is highly decorated but dark and grim, while the interior is dull in comparison but quite light and pretty. The **Methodist church**, dating from 1841, also has a fine interior, with a circular balcony. Its construction was financed largely through the efforts of freed slaves. There is a little bell tower at the south end, erected in 1907.

Places outside the centre

Botanical Gardens ⓘ *http://nationalparks.gov.vc, daily 0600-1800, US$2 entrance, US$4 guide, no smoking, no alcohol, no loud music,* just below Government House and the Prime Minister's residence, are well worth a visit and are the oldest in the Western Hemisphere (see box, above). The gardens are compact and unfortunately the plants are not labelled, which forces you to take a guide to learn about them. There is a certain amount of hassling for business by the guides, particularly if a cruise ship is in port. **Nicholas Wildlife Complex** has parrots, agouti, Barbados green monkey and St Vincent parrot, but they aren't very well housed. The gardens are about a 20-minute walk from the market square: go along Grenville Street, past the cathedrals, turn right into Bentinck Square, right again and continue uphill to the gate. Or take a bus, EC$1 from the terminal.

Fort Charlotte ① *T784-4561060, Mon-Fri 0800-1500, open weekends if a cruise ship is in port, EC$5/US$2, but no one collects the fee, guides available for a tip,* is on the promontory on the north side of Kingstown Bay, 636 ft above sea level, a 15-minute drive out of town (EC$1.50 from bus terminal to village below from where it is a steep walk, if you ask the driver he might take you into the fort for EC$1-2, worth it if it is hot, or take a taxi). Although the fort, completed in 1805, was designed to fend off attacks from the sea, the main threat was the Black Caribs and many of its 34 guns (some of which are still in place) and the moat therefore faced inland. In 1779 the Black Caribs had joined forces with a French invasion party to take St Vincent and had burned sugar plantations and attacked the white English colonists. The British did not want a repeat of the violence. The gatehouse, 1806, was where Major Champion of the Royal Scots Fusiliers was killed on 13 October 1824 (see plaque in St George's Cathedral) by Private Ballasty. The murderer was executed at the scene of the crime. In the old barrack rooms, a series of paintings shows the early history of St Vincent. Painted by William Linzest Prescott in 1972, they suffer from poor lighting and their condition is deteriorating. There is also a coastguard lookout which controls the comings and goings of ships entering the port. The views are wonderful on a clear day, looking along the chain of Grenadine islands. Below, the ruins of a military hospital can be seen, as well as a bathing pool at sea level on the end of the point, used when the fort housed people suffering from yaws. Part of the fort is used as a women's prison and the moat is their exercise yard.

Leeward Coast → *For listings, see pages 90-99.*

The Leeward Highway is a dramatic drive along the west coast towards La Soufrière; there are lush valleys and magnificent seaviews. It is a very crumpled landscape and the road is steep and twisty.

Leaving Kingstown
The road leaves Kingstown and initially heads inland. There are views down into Campden Park Bay, to a deep water port complex and flour mill. The road passes through the small village of **Questelles** before rejoining the coast briefly at **Buccament Bay** and down into **Layou** where there are a few excellent examples of gingerbread houses.

Natural disasters

In 1902, La Soufrière erupted, killing 2000 people, just two days before Mont Pelée erupted on Martinique, killing 30,000. Much of the farming land was seriously damaged and economic conditions, already extremely poor, deteriorated further. 1979, the year St Vincent gained independence from Great Britain, is also remembered for the eruption of La Soufrière on Good Friday, 13 April. Fortunately no one was killed as thousands were evacuated, but there was considerable agricultural damage. In 1980 Hurricane Allen caused further devastation to the plantations and it took years for production of crops such as coconuts and bananas to recover. Hurricane Emily destroyed an estimated 70% of the banana crop in 1987. Christmas 2013 brought death and destruction on a par with some of the worst hurricanes St Vincent has known. A low-level trough system brought severe rains and high winds which caused floods and landslides in St Vincent and the Grenadines, Saint Lucia and Dominica 23-25 December. St Vincent reported nine deaths and over 500 people affected, of whom 237 were provided with emergency shelter. Dozens of homes were destroyed and hundreds damaged. The Government declared a level two disaster, meaning that the damage was severe and specialized external assistance was requested. The Leeward side of the island bore the brunt of the storm with rivers bursting their banks and sweeping all before them. The Buccament River flooded the Buccament Bay Resort, the property was covered with debris and mud and the beach was washed away. The Cumberland watershed was also badly hit and the hydroelectric plant knocked out, while residential areas were also flooded. Many areas were without clean water and power for some time.

About a mile after Questelles look for the Vermont Nature Trail sign, then turn right up the Buccament Valley to Peniston and Vermont. The car park at 975 ft is close to the Vermont Nature Centre within the St Vincent Parrot Reserve.

Vermont Nature Trail and St Vincent Parrot Reserve
ⓘ *Daily 0700-1700, visitor centre and other facilities open from 0900, EC$5/US$2. Buses from Kingston go to Peniston from where it is a long walk.*
This is an area of great biodiversity with both primary and secondary rainforest providing a habitat for the St Vincent parrot and lots of other birds, lizards, opossum, agouti and the endemic Congo snake (harmless). There is a marvellous two-mile trail and, unless you want scientific information, a guide is not necessary; get a trail map from the visitor centre. There is a rest stop at 1350 ft, and a Parrot

Lookout Platform at 1450 ft, probably the best place to see the St Vincent parrot. Be prepared for rain, mosquitoes and chiggars, and use insect repellent.

Layou Petroglyph Park

ⓘ *Mon-Sat 0900-1600, EC$5/US$2 to use the facilities and US$1 for the toilets. The visitor centre is basically a room with some photos on the walls, but no cafe. There are picnic spots and a bathing pool in the Rutland River.*

There are some interesting **petroglyphs** and **rock carvings** dating back to the Siboney, Arawak and Carib eras. The best known are just north of Layou at this park, carved on a huge boulder, about 20 ft wide, next to a stream, which are believed to date from AD 300-600 during the Saladoid, or Arawak, occupation of the island. It has been speculated that the largest drawing is of Yocahú, their principal male god, yoca being the word for cassava and hú meaning 'giver of'. It is believed that the tribes of the Lesser Antilles, including St Vincent, associated this deity's power to provide cassava with the mystery of the volcanoes, since their carvings are conical. The Yocahú cult was wiped out by the invading Caribs before the arrival of the Europeans, but could have existed from about AD200. Look for a signpost north of the village which takes you to a reception building and the trail down to the river. A bit further down the river but still in the park are the ruins of an old indigo factory.

Barrouallie

Passing Mount Wynne and Peter's Hope, Barrouallie is the next village of any size. It is a fishing village and on the beach are fishing boats, nets, pigs and chickens scratching about. The local speciality catch is 'black fish', in reality a short-finned pilot whale, which grows to about 18 ft. Here, in the playground of the Anglican secondary school, there is a petroglyph dated at 800 BC, known as the **Ogham Stone**. One theory claims that it is in Celtic script. If the children are not in class they will highlight the picture in white chalk for you.

Wallilabou Bay

The road also passes through the remains of a sugar mill (the furnace chimney is still standing) and then heads inland from the popular anchorage and restaurant at Wallilabou Bay. A stone gateway marks the entrance to the **Wallilabou Falls** (Wally-la-boo), or Wallilabou Heritage Park ⓘ *daily 0800-1700, EC$5/US$2, restaurant, changing rooms, gazebo.* Large samaan trees give shade to the area and keep it cool. The waterfall is small but it can give you quite a pressure shower and you can bathe in the pool. The park was once a plantation and the remains of a stone wall cross the river. On the opposite side of the road is a nutmeg plantation.

Wallilabou Bay was one of the settings for the *Pirates of the Caribbean* movies, *Curse of the Black Pearl* and *Dead Man's Chest*, with copies of 18th-century piers and storage houses being built here to replicate Port Royal in Jamaica. Many of the Grenadine islands were also used for location shooting, including Union Island, the Tobago Cays and Petit Tabac, where Captain Sparrow and Elizabeth were marooned by Barbossa at the end of the film. Unfortunately, the film set has not been maintained and each storm destroys a bit more of the props so it is becoming increasingly dilapidated.

Cumberland Bay and around

The road goes inland along the **Wallilabou Valley** before quickly rising over the ridge into the North Leeward district. Another pretty beach is reached at Cumberland. Cumberland Bay is popular with people on yachts, partly because it is so attractive and partly because the bay is deep and boats can anchor close to shore. **Cumberland Beach Recreational Park** has a welcome centre, restaurant (0700-2100, later on Sat with karaoke) and bar, toilets, showers (EC$5/US$2), laundry (0700-1900), jetty, water, ice and internet.

Another attraction inland from here is the **Cumberland Nature Trail** ① *daily 0700-1700, EC$5/US$2, visitor centre, ticket booth, toilets and parking at the start of the trail*, which meanders through the rainforest of the Cumberland Forest Reserve in the Upper Cumberland Valley for 1.6 miles. It is very good for birdwatching and there are hides along the trail where you can watch for the St Vincent parrot, whistling warbler, brown trembler, tanagers, fly-catchers and many other birds. Birdwatching guides are available on request. From Grove, where it starts, the trail follows a wooden water pipe taking water to three hydroelectricity plants on the Cumberland River. Some parts of the trail are steep and overgrown, becoming slippery and dangerous if it rains.

From Cumberland the road climbs quickly to **Coulls Hill** with perhaps the best view on the coast. The road is most attractive through **Chateaubelair** (Port of Entry, restaurant, use their facilities to change for a swim and have a snack), skirting Petit Bordel (drugs-financed speed boats on the beach) with small islands offshore, to **Richmond** and **Wallibou beach**. There are some beach facilities at Wallibou and these are beautiful black sand beaches. The road ends here.

Dark View Falls and further north

① *Daily 0900-1700, EC$5/US$2, ticket booth at start of trail, parking, food kiosk.*
Inland, on a tributary of Richmond River, are these falls, which consist of two cascades, one above the other, plunging down cliff faces into pools. The hike through the rainforest to the first one is easy and short, crossing the Richmond River on a bamboo suspension bridge or a more conventional bridge and passing through a bamboo grove. There are gazebos, a changing room, picnic area and viewing platform. The trail up steps and across the river on slippery rocks to the second waterfall is more difficult, but doesn't take long. A quiet and peaceful spot most of the time and exquisitely beautiful, the water is

cold and refreshing and the falls' water pressure will leave your skin tingling. Swimming is better in the upper pool.

One of the most popular excursions on the island was a boat trip to the **Falls of Baleine** on the northwest coast. It was possible to climb up the side behind the falls and jump into the natural swimming pool below, which entertained thrill-seekers. Unfortunately, a serious rock fall blocking the trail to the falls upriver, and the chance of another one, means that the site is closed indefinitely.

Windward Coast → *For listings, see pages 90-99.*

Kingstown to the coast

The Queens Drive takes you into the hills south of Kingstown and gives splendid views all around. The Marriaqua Valley with its numerous streams is particularly beautiful and you can get a glorious view from the **Belmont Lookout** ① *daily 0800-1730, free, toilets EC$2*, over lush farmland, forests and the sea as far as Bequia. This area is often referred to as the island's 'breadbasket' and you will see plots of bananas, nutmeg, cocoa, breadfruit, coconut and a variety of provisions (root crops). The highest point is the **Bonhomme Mountain** (3192 ft, 973 m) which overlooks the valley and streams tumble down and merge to flow over the rocks of the Yambou Gorge before heading out to sea.

In the valley, beyond Mesopotamia (commonly known as Mespo), the lush, tropical gardens of **Montreal Estate** ① *T4581198, www.montrealestgdns.f9.co.uk, Mon-Fri, Dec-Aug 0900-1700, closed holidays, EC$5*, are worth a visit where anthuriums are grown commercially for the domestic market. The owner, Timothy Vaughn, is a well-known landscape gardener in Europe and this is his first tropical garden, full of organic flowers and colourful foliage, with glorious views of Argyll and Mesopotamia Valley. It is designed in three sections, one of which includes a wild garden leading down to a river and a pool where you can swim. Take your time to explore the winding paths; there are exotic plants around every bend.

Windward Highway to Black Point

The road meets the **Windward Highway** at Peruvian Vale. It gets progressively drier as the road goes north hugging yellow sandstone cliffs which contrast with the white waves surging in towards the black volcanic beaches. A number of banana packaging stations are passed especially around **Colonarie**.

Black Point Tunnel is 350 ft long and was constructed by Colonel Thomas Browne using Carib and African slaves in 1815. It was blasted through volcanic rock from one bay to the other and the drill holes are still visible, as are storage rooms and recesses for candles. It is very atmospheric and there are a few bats as well as people washing in the water which pours out of the rock. It provided an important link with the sugar estates in the north and sugar was hauled through

Arrowroot

St Vincent's history as an arrowroot producer goes back to the days of the Amerindians, when it was used as a food and medicine. Archaeological studies have revealed evidence of arrowroot cultivation going back 7000 years and it is believed that the name comes from the Arawak word aru-aru (meal of meals). As well as it being a staple foodstuff, it was also used to draw out poison from poison-arrow wounds. It became important in colonial trade in the first half of the 20th century, reaching 50% of total exports, filling the void left by the decline of the sugar industry, but it has since been supplanted by the growth of bananas. You can still see evidence of the industry with factory ruins around the island but cultivation is now mostly in the north east, around Owia where many people are of Kalinago descent. Output is a fraction of its height in the 1960s when it was the principal source of employment and income for rural Vincentians. The harvest takes place from October to May, when the rhizome is broken off from the shoot and the latter then replanted at the same time. There are processing plants at Belle Vue and Owia. As well as its use as a starch in cooking, arrowroot is also used in the paper industry, cosmetics and pharmaceuticals.

the tunnel to be loaded on to boats in Byera Bay. Black sand Byera Beach is the longest in St Vincent and the sea is rough, but in the days of the sugar plantations the coast curved round more giving protection to shipping and there was a jetty.

You cannot see the tunnel from the road, which goes over the top. Turn towards the sea between the gas station and the river down a dirt road which leads to Black Point Recreation Site (where cricket is played and people gather for Easter Monday celebrations). Now known as **Black Point Heritage and Recreational Park** ① 0700-1730, EC$5/US$2, it comprises the tunnel, beach, Grand Sable River and recreational Field. It was also another film location for Pirates of the Caribbean: Curse of the Black Pearl. Do not swim in the sea here.

Georgetown to the far north

Georgetown was the first capital of the island and is now the second largest town after Kingstown. For many years it was economically depressed after the loss of sea cotton and arrowroot and then problems with bananas. However, the area is now picking up and you can see many new or refurbished homes. It is not a tourist destination but there are places to eat and drink if you are passing through.

The road to **Sandy Bay** (beyond Georgetown), where St Vincent's remaining Black Caribs live, is now good. However, you have to cross the Rabacca Dry

Yo ho ho!

The largest company in the Georgetown area is St Vincent Distillers Ltd, which produces four rum brands and a rum punch. There has been a rum distillery on the site since the late 19th century, although its fortunes have fluctuated widely. The current structure dates from the 1920s when it was built by the Mt Bentinck Estate and had access to molasses from the sugar factory next door. In 1963, the year the sugar mill closed and bananas replaced sugar cane on the hillsides, it was sold to the government and became St Vincent Distillers Ltd. Molasses were then imported. Twenty years later there was a flurry of interest in renewing the sugar industry. A new crop of sugar cane was planted; the sugar mill was refurbished with equipment from Trinidad and new distillation equipment came from the UK. However, by the time the new distillery produced its first rum in 1985, the sugar mill had already closed again and bananas had reasserted their dominance over the landscape. The government sold the company in 1996 to CK Greaves & Co Ltd. St Vincent Distillers Ltd has continued to produce world-class rums and win international awards, most recently gold at the World Drinks Awards in 2014, when its Captain Bligh XO was adjudged the World's Best Rum and World's Best Gold Rum, while its Sunset Very Strong Rum won a bronze medal for Best Overproof Rum. In their comments about Captain Bligh, the judges noted that the "delicate rum shows a lovely balance of light wood, providing vanillas and a hint of cocoa." Sunset is the local favourite and the downfall of many an unsuspecting tourist at 48 over proof, 84.5% alcohol by volume.

River, a jumble of rocks, grit, rubbish and dead wood swept down from the mountains above, which sometimes is not dry and therefore not passable. Rocks and sand are extracted for the building industry. Sandy Bay is poor but beyond it is an even poorer village along a rough dirt road, **Owia**. Here is **Salt Pond Park** ⓘ *0900-1800, EC$5/US$2, toilets, showers, gazebos, playground, picnic area*, a natural area of tidal pools filled with small marine life and reef fish. The rough Atlantic crashes around the huge boulders and lava formations, then trickles into the protected pools and it is very picturesque. The villagers have planted gardens and made 217 steps down to the Salt Pond area. There is also an arrowroot processing factory which can be visited.

Past Owia is **Fancy**, the poorest village on the island, also Black Carib and very isolated, reached by a rough jeep track which makes a nice walk. Baleine Falls (see above) are a two-mile hike from here around the tip of the island, rugged and not for the unadventurous. Fishing boats can be hired in Fancy to collect you (do not pay in advance). The falls are, however, closed indefinitely due to a serious rockfall.

The airport is just southeast of Kingstown at Arnos Vale, a residential area where there is also a sports complex. The road runs round the runway and down towards the coast at Indian Bay. There are several hotels in this area, stretching along the seafront to Calliaqua Bay. It is very pleasant, with light sand beaches, Young Island just offshore, Bequia in the distance and dozens of moored yachts. Many people stay here rather than in the capital, as it is an easy commute into Kingstown if you need to go in, while there are marinas, dive shops, the best restaurants and water sports facilities here. This part of the island is drier and has different vegetation and birdlife.

Leeward side

St Vincent has splendid, safe beaches on the Leeward side, most of which have volcanic black sand. The lightest coloured sand can be found on the south coast in the **Villa area**, where there are several hotels, water sports and marinas. At **Sunsail Lagoon** in **Calliaqua** there is a lovely long, crescent-shaped beach, **Canash**, which is perfect for young children. Further round the rocks, there are two more beaches becoming progressively more golden the closer to the point you get. Just offshore is **Young Island** (see Where to stay, below), which has a small, golden sand, 'improved' beach.

Next to Young Island, **Fort Duvernette** ⓘ *EC$5/US$2, accessible by water taxi from the jetty at Villa Mon-Sat,* also known as 'rock fort' and previously as Young's Sugar Loaf, has gun emplacements on top of a volcanic plug in the sea overlooking Calliaqua Bay and Indian Bay. The guns were to protect commercial shipping, principally the sugar trade and cargo bound for Britain. A staircase winds up the rockface to two gun decks where you can find cannon from the reigns of both George II and George III, as well as the remains of buildings.

Windward side

The Windward Coast is rockier with rolling surf and strong currents, making it dangerous for swimming. **Brighton Salt Pond Beach** has lovely swimming conditions most days and magically clear water. Cruise ships sometimes bring their guests here. All beaches are public. Some are difficult to reach by road, but boat trips can be arranged to the less accessible beauty spots such as **Breakers Beach**, Prospect.

North of Brighton on the east coast, **Rawacou Recreational Park** ⓘ *daily 0800-1700, EC$5/US$2, parking, food and drink stalls, gazebos, toilets, changing rooms, fire pits, stage and entertainment centre, volleyball court,* straddles a rocky promontory with a dark sand beach on either side. Coconut palms and seagrape trees line the shore, but this is the Atlantic and you should not swim in the sea. There is a man-made pool for swimming.

The new international airport is being built at **Argyle**, on the Windward Coast, with the runway parallel to the sea. Construction work uncovered forgotten ruins and a new heritage park will have as its centrepiece the old sugar mill at **Escape Estate**, which had been swallowed up by forest. The mill was water-driven and the water wheel is still there. Other ruined buildings are to be restored to make a working museum of St Vincent's agricultural history. The heritage park will also include the Yambou 1 petroglyphs, which have been relocated half a mile from the original site because of the airport construction. St Vincent and the Grenadines National Trust is working with archaeologists from Egypt, Australia and Cuba on both projects to preserve the island's heritage in the face of developmental demands. Replicas of the rock drawings are on display at the Carnegie Building in Kingstown, see page 79.

● St Vincent listings

For hotel and restaurant price codes and other relevant information, see pages 13-16.

● Where to stay

Kingstown *p76, map p79*
$$$ Cobblestone Inn, Upper Bay St, T784-4561937, http:// thecobblestoneinn.com. Upstairs in a charming building dating from 1814 which used to be a sugar and arrowroot warehouse. 24 rooms and 6 suites, renovated to highlight Georgian architecture, good, with a/c, TV, rooftop restaurant and bar for breakfast, lunch and dinner.
$$$ Grenadine House, Kingstown Park, T784-4581800, www.grenadine house.com. Originally the governor's residence and the oldest guesthouse on the island, but completely modernized as a 20-room boutique hotel. Comfortable, good Wi-Fi, with views of the garden or mountains, quite a walk into town. Pool, bar,

restaurant, indoor or outdoor dining with a view to the sea.
$$$ Haddon, McKies Hill, T784-4561897, www.haddonhotel.com. Good for business travellers, within walking distance of the centre but away from the bustle, large rooms and suites with Wi-Fi and work desk, business centre and conference facilities, good restaurant and bar, friendly and efficient service.
$$$ New Montrose Hotel, New Montrose, T784-4570172, www.new montrosehotel.com. 25 rooms, studios and apartments, 1-2 bedrooms, balcony, some kitchenettes, a/c, Wi-Fi, view of Kingstown and Grenadines, close to Botanical Gardens and short walk to a good supermarket.

Leeward Coast *p82, map p77*
$$$$ Buccament Bay, T44-(0)1268 242463, www.buccamentbay.com. A luxury, all-inclusive resort at the mouth of the Buccament River, which

flooded in 2013, see box, page 83, but is now back in full operation. Garden or beachfront villas with lots of facilities and plunge pools. Good for families, lots of activities and sports including football, yoga, tennis, rugby, dive shop on site, excellent and efficient service. Very good food and drinks, including delicious smoothies and speciality beverages.

The south *p89, map p77*
$$$$ Young Island, T784-4584826, www.youngisland.com. A tiny, privately owned islet, 200 yd off the coast at Villa. 29 cottages, some plunge pools, spa treatments, meal packages available, tennis, part sailing, diving, wedding and honeymoon packages offered. There is a lovely lagoon swimming pool, surrounded by tropical flowers and a golden-sand beach overlooking Indian Bay.
$$$$-$$$ Beachcombers Hotel, Villa Beach, T784-4584283, www.beach combershotel.com. Small, family-run and on the beach, variety of rooms and suites, the cheaper ones being quite small and basic, the more costly ones really nice, restaurant and bar, food 0700-2200, bar open later, happy hour 1700-1830, Sat night barbecue with steel band, spa, Wi-Fi, friendly service.
$$$$-$$$ Grand View Beach, Villa Point, 3 miles from town, close to Arnos Vale airport, T784-4584811, www.grandviewhotel.com. A former cotton plantation house in grounds of 8 acres on elevated position overlooking the marinas and yachts, the hotel has aged gracefully and service has charm, 19 rooms, pool,

tennis, squash, fully equipped gym, yoga, pilates, aerobics, massage, excursions arranged, 2 restaurants, excellent breakfast in dining room with view, steps down to **Grand View Grill** for evening meal, room service. Wi-Fi in reception area.
$$$$-$$$ Mariners Hotel, Villa Bay, T784-4574000, www.marinershotel. com. 20 rooms on the beach, a/c, room service, Wi-Fi, TV, comfortable, jetty overlooks Young Island, **French Verandah** restaurant for lunch and dinner, Fri night barbecues, dive packages arranged. Boardwalk to larger beach and other hotels and their restaurants.
$$$$-$$$ Sunset Shores, Villa Beach, T784-4584411, www.sunset shores.com. Beachfront hotel in 3 acres of gardens, spacious rooms, price depends on view, a/c, TV, Wi-Fi, restaurant and bar, Sat night barbecue. Pleasant staff, lovely location.
$$$ Paradise Beach, Villa Beach, T784-5700000, www.paradisesvg.com. Small hotel with comfortable rooms and good beds, a/c, fans, Wi-Fi and cell phone with each room. Beachfront rooms have the best view of the sunset and yachts looking over to Young Island. Good restaurant serving traditional local dishes and a popular Fri night barbecue. On bus route from Kingstown to airport, EC$1.50, or taxi to airport EC$30. **Fantasea Tours** is under same ownership as hotel for trips to Tobago Cays and other Grenadine islands.
$$$ Tranquillity Beach, Indian Bay, T784-4584021, www.tranquillityhotel. com. Excellent view, 1-, 2-, 3-bedroom

apartments by the beach, some apartments up flight of steps, no frills but great value for the location, a/c, kitchen facilities, fans, TV, laundry service, massages, clean, friendly, very helpful owner, Lucelle Providence.

$$$ Villa Lodge Hotel, Villa Point, T784-4584641, www.villalodge.com. 11 rooms and 8, 1- or 2-bedroom fully equipped apartments overlooking Indian Bay, discounts for longer stay, a/c, fans, TV, Wi-Fi, pool with lovely view, restaurant, bar, meal plans available. Next to **Grand View** where, for a fee, you can use their gym and sports facilities.

$$ Sea Breeze Guesthouse, Arnos Vale, near airport, T784-4584969, seabreezetours@vincysurf.com. Run by the Daize family, Hal Daize operates **Sea Breeze Nature Tours**. 6 rooms with bath share 2 kitchenettes and sitting room with TV, noisy, friendly, helpful, bus to town or airport from the door.

⊘ Restaurants

Kingstown *p76, map p79*

$$$ Basil's Bar and Restaurant (see below) has a branch beside the **Cobblestone Inn**, in Upper Bay St, T784-4572713. Mon-Sat 0800-2400. Buffet Mon-Fri 1200-1400 for hungry people, acceptable but not startling, also à la carte lunch and dinner, pleasant for an evening drink and a chat.

$$$-$$ Bounty Restaurant and Art Gallery, Egmont St, upstairs, T784-4561776. Mon-Fri 0730-1700, Sat 0730-1330. The oldest restaurant in town, windows open to catch the breeze,

breakfast and lunch, patties, rotis, cakes and pastries, iced coffee/tea.

$$$-$$ Ras Ital, Paul's Av. Mon-Fri lunch. Rastafarian restaurant serving mostly vegetarian dishes but also some meat and fish. A few daily specials to choose from for lunch, fresh juices, mauby and teas. From Halifax St walk past the Court House on your right, then take your next right. At the end of the road, turn left and Ras Ital is on the right.

$$$-$$ Time Out Cafe, at the cruise ship terminal, T784-4571350, see facebook. Popular with locals and cruise ship passengers, British-run, friendly service. Good all-day English breakfast, a decent cup of coffee (imported), extensive menu for food and drinks including local specialities. Also popular after hours with karaoke and themed nights such as Indian curry buffet or Latin nights. Free Wi-Fi but ask for the code.

$$$-$$ Vee-Jay's, Lower Bay St, T784-4572845. Mon-Sat 0900-2000, Fri until late with live band. Friendly and offers good, wholesome local food, best rotis in town. Great place for lunch, good local juices, cocktail bar, entrées EC$12-45, great steel band, karaoke at weekends.

Leeward Coast *p82, map p77*

$$$-$$ Wallilabou Anchorage, T784-4587270, www.wallilabou.com. From 0800 for breakfast, lunch and dinner. Caters mainly for yachties, mooring facilities, West Indian specialities, chicken, fish or veg lunch, juices, internet access, also 12-room hotel overlooking bay. Site of much of the filming for the 3 *Pirates of the Caribbean* movies, see the poster of Johnny Depp in the ladies' restroom.

$$ Beach Front Restaurant & Bar, Chateaubelair, T784-4582853. Lunch and dinner. Eat inside or outdoors, roof terrace with shade, good view of bay, rotis and fish meals for lunch, happy hour Fri, there can be a swell here so if you are on a yacht it is sometimes better to stop at Wallilabou.

$$ Bush Bar, Queensbury, Vermont, T784-4918127, zenpunnett@gmail.com. Up in the hills near the Vermont Nature Trails, Zen uses organic food from her own garden or neighbouring farmers to produce wholesome meals and drinks, served under rustic bamboo and thatch surrounded by birds, butterflies and pets. Popular with locals and tourists venturing off the beaten track. Zen also rents a delightful cottage which is close to nature but a step up from camping.

Windward Coast *p86, map p77*
$$ Ferdie's Footsteps, on the main street in Georgetown, on the corner with Cambridge St, T784-4586433. Daily breakfast, lunch and early dinner. Food and drinks, popular with volcano hikers, great fish and roasted breadfruit.

The south *p89, map p77*
The best restaurants are usually in the hotels, eg the upscale **French Verandah** at **Mariner's Hotel**, or Wilkie's at **Grand View Beach Hotel**.
$$$ Black Pearl, Blue Lagoon Marina, T784-5302846, mockingbird330@outlook.com. On the waterfront,

convenient for yachts, popular with sailors, good food, local ingredients, excellent fish, free Wi-Fi.

$$ Surfside Beachbar/Restaurant, the former Club Iguana at Villa, T784-4575362. Tue-Sun 1000-2200. Informal Continental/West Indian, mainly known for the very good pizza. Good bar too with happy hour 1830-1930 Fri, Sat.

❶ Bars and clubs

St Vincent *p75, map p77*
Many hotels and restaurants have live music in the evenings. This may be a steel band in conjunction with a barbecue. Check for happy hours at bars for lower-priced drinks, snacks and often entertainment.

Attic, Melville St. 1700 till late. Upstairs in an old stone building, live entertainment several nights a week, jazz, karaoke, dancing, large screen video, music bar. Very popular with locals.

Culture Pot Square, Calliaqua. Fri from 2000. A form of street party in the beach area, where you can find music and food, singing, karaoke, and dancing, arts and crafts.

Flow Wine Bar, Allen Building upstairs, James St, Kingstown, T784-4570809, www.flowwinebar.com. Mon-Fri 1100-2200, Sat 1800-late. Pleasant setting indoors or on rooftop terrace bar. Tue tapas evening with 4 substantial tapas paired with 4 glasses of wine, good and very popular. Varied menu at other times too for lunch or dinner. Good and extensive wine list but also their own home-brewed beer which makes a change from Hairoun, as well as spirits, coffee, teas.

Flowt Beach Bar, Blue Lagoon Marina, Ratho Mill, T784-4568435, see facebook. Same company as **Flow Wine Bar**, good food, good burgers, drinks and hospitality. DJ on Sat.

🎭 Entertainment

St Vincent *p75, map p77*
Casino
Emerald Valley Casino, Peniston Valley, T784-4567824. Wed-Mon 2100-0300. Call for transport, low key casino with bar, Ladies' Night Wed.

Cinema
Russell's Cinema, Stoney Ground, T784-4579308, www.russells-cinema.com.

○ Shopping

St Vincent *p75, map p77*
Arts and crafts
Fibres and flowers are the raw materials for much traditional craft and modern art work. Bamboo, banana fibre, palm leaves, grass and flower petals are crafted into hats, mats, slippers, toys, baskets and pictures. Conch shell galleons, egg shell mosaics, coconut helicopters, clothing and shoes, steel pans, goatskin drums, books by and about Vincentians, jewellery, carnival dolls and a variety of wood carvings can also be found. Crafts can be found in Kingstown upstairs at the Vegetable Market or at the Craft Outlet in Frenches. On the Leeward Coast, Fibreworks, in the Buccament Valley at Penniston, founded by British-trained artist Vonnie Roudette, use local materials to make crafts reflecting the local environment and people. Also on the Leeward Coast is the Wallilabou Craft Centre, a co-operative where training is provided in various techniques of straw and weaving using fibres from pandanas and wiss plants to make baskets, handbags, hats and toys.

Noah's Arkade, Blue Caribbean Building, Bay St, Kingstown, T784-4571513. For handicrafts, resort wear and books.

Nzimbu Arts & Craft, McKies Hill, T784-4571677, www.nzimbu-browne.com. Goat-skin drums, batik and banana-leaf artwork, Nzimbu is often found on Bay St on Fri, selling his crafts on the roadside. He is also a musician, favouring calypso and rapso styles in his recordings.

Food
CK Greaves & Co Ltd, T784-4571074, www.ckgreaves.com. A well-stocked chain of supermarkets with stores on Upper Bay St, Kingstown, Mon-Thu 0800-1700, Fri 0800-1900, Sat 0700-1300, **Sunrise Supermarket & Bakery**, Arnos Vale, Mon-Thu 0745-2000, Fri 0745-2100, Sat 0700-2000, Sun 800-1200, and **Greaves Marketplace** in Pembroke, Mon-Thu 0900-1900, Fri 0900-2000, Sat 0800-2000, Sun 0900-1300.
Gourmet Food, Calliaqua, T784-4562983, also on Bequia. Gourmet provisions.
Kingstown market (do not take photos of the vendors) for excellent fresh fruit and vegetables.
Super J, www.superjsupermarkets.com/stvincent supermarket at Russell

Diving in St Vincent and the Grenadines

The underwater wildlife around St Vincent and the Grenadines is varied and beautiful. There are many types and colours of coral, including black coral at a depth of only 30 ft in places. On the New Guinea Reef (Petit Byahaut) you can find three types of black coral in six different colours. The coral is protected so do not remove any. There are 10 marine protected areas including the northeast coast of St Vincent (and the Devil's Table in Bequia, Isle à Quatre, all Mustique, the east coast of Canouan, all of Mayreau, the Tobago Cays, the whole of Palm Island, Petit St Vincent and the surrounding reefs). Spearfishing is strictly forbidden to visitors and no one is allowed to spear a lobster. Buying lobster out of season (1 May-30 September) is illegal as is buying a female lobster with eggs. Fishing for your own consumption is allowed outside the protected areas. Contact the **Fisheries Department**, T4562738, for more information on rules and regulations.

There is reef diving, wall diving, drift diving and wrecks to explore. The St Vincent reefs are fairly deep, at 55-90 ft, so scuba diving is more rewarding than snorkelling. Dive sites include Bottle Reef, the Forest, the Garden, New Guinea Reef and the Wall. In Kingstown Harbour there are three wrecks at one site, the Semistrand, another cargo freighter and an ancient wreck stirred up by Hurricane Hugo, as well as two cannons, a large anchor and several bathtubs.

Shopping Centre, Stoney Ground, Kingstown, T784-4572984, Mon-Thu 0700-2100, Fri-Sat 1900-2200, Sun and holidays 0700-1300, and at Arnos Vale, T784-4572981, Mon-Sat 0700-2200, Sun 0700-1500, holidays 0700-1300. Both have delis and ATMs.

⏲ What to do

St Vincent *p75, map p77*
Cricket
Test Match cricket ground at the Arnos Vale Sports Complex, near the airport. St Vincent was not chosen as one of the venues for the 2007 Cricket World Cup, but 4 warm-up matches were played there. It is one of the most picturesque grounds in the world with a view of the Grenadines and was extensively refurbished in 2006-2007 to give it a capacity of 15,000, with an operations centre, a large players' pavilion and media centre. Alongside there are netball and tennis courts.

Diving
Dive St Vincent (Bill Tewes) at Young Island Dock, T784-4574714, www.divestvincent.com. Set up in 1978, benefits from a wealth of local knowledge and experience. NAUI, PADI certification courses, equipment and camera rental, lots of packages available, including accommodation at several hotels. Specializes in small groups.

Indigo Dive, **Buccament Bay Hotel**, T784-4939494, www.indigodive.com. Single-tank dive US$75, 2-tank dive US$135, night dive surcharge US$25 to cover light hire, PADI Open Water course US$600, 1½-hr snorkelling or glass-bottom boat tour, US$45. **Buccament Bay Hotel** guests take priority so bookings from others need at least 24 hrs' advance notice.

Sailing

Barefoot Yacht Charters, Blue Lagoon, T784-4569526, www.barefoot yachts.com. An American Sailing Association (ASA) sailing school and the longest-established charter company, offering bareboat or crewed yachts and catamarans. Owned by the Barnard family, who also own **SVG Air**. **Horizon Yacht Charters**, Blue Lagoon Marina, T1-866-4637245 toll free, 1-473-4391000 in Grenada, www. horizonyachtcharters.com. Allow a one-way charter so you start your charter in Blue Lagoon, St Vincent and sail down to True Blue Bay in Grenada, or vice versa, for an extra fee. They also have bases in the British Virgin Islands, Antigua and Sint Maarten. **TMM Bareboat Vacations**, Blue Lagoon, T784-4569608, www.sailtmm. com. Bareboat or crewed yachts and catamarans of 38-51 ft, also offer one-way charter to Grenada.

Spectator sports

Victoria Park Stadium, Kingstown, hosts sporting events such as athletics and soccer/football. The national soccer team is called **Vincy Heat**. The national rugby team is called **Amazonia**

Guildingii after the endemic parrot and they wear green, yellow and blue, the colours of the bird and the national flag. Other major sports on St Vincent are basketball, netball, tennis, squash and cycling. For more information contact the **National Sports Council**, T784-4584201, svgnsc@vincysurf. com; **SVG Football Federation**, T784-4561092, svgfootball@vincysurf.com; **SVG National Rugby Team**, T784-4333334, svgrufc@vincysurf.com.

Squash

Cecil Cyrus Squash Complex, St James Place, Kingstown, reservations T784-4561805. **Grand View Beach Hotel** and the **Prospect Racquet Club**, T784-4584866.

Surfing

Surfing is good on the reef off **Lagoon Bay** (Canash) and at **Shipping Bay** and **Argyle** on the Windward Coast for strong surfers.

Tennis

Many of the more expensive hotels have tennis courts but there are others at the **Kingstown Tennis Club** and the **Prospect Racquet Club**. Buccament Bay Hotel has the **Pat Cash Tennis Club**. The **National Tennis Centre** with a club house and floodlit courts have been built in Calliaqua, contact **SVG Tennis Association**, T784-4574090, for reservations. Take the road opposite Howards Marine before the bridge.

Tour operators

Fantasea Tours, at **Villa Beach**, T784-4574477, www.fantaseatours.com.

Hiking on St Vincent

The highest peak on the island, La Soufrière volcano, rises to about 4000 ft. In 1902, La Soufrière erupted, killing 2000 people. In 1970 an island reared up out of the lake in the crater; it smokes and the water round it is very warm. Hiking to the volcano is very popular, but you must leave very early in the morning and allow a full day for the trip. Non-resident visitors are required by the National Parks, Rivers and Beaches Authority to use the services of an approved tour guide. Take water and insect repellent and wear good shoes. About two miles north of Georgetown (van from Kingstown to Georgetown EC$4, you can ask the driver to make a detour to the start of the trail for an extra charge) on the Windward side you cross the Rabacca Dry River, then take a left fork and walk/drive through banana plantations to where the trail begins. It takes about three hours to reach the crater edge and it is a strenuous hike along a marked trail, the first three miles are through the Rabacca plantation, then up, along Bamboo Ridge and all the way to the crater's magnificent edge; the top can be cloudy, windy, cold and rainy, take adequate clothing and footwear. There is an alternative, unmarked and even more challenging four-hour route from the leeward side starting from the end of the road after Richmond, but you will need a guide. There are guided tours which start on the windward side and end on the leeward side, about six or seven hours, with the advantage that you are met at your destination by the driver and do not have to worry about scarce public transport. Leave an extra set of clothes in the van in case you get wet through.

An easier climb is up Mount St Andrew, near Kingstown. A tarmac track runs up to the radio mast on the summit of the peak, at 2413 ft, passing first through banana and vegetable gardens and then through forest. There are no parrots but it is particularly good for the Antillean crested hummingbird and black hawks. To reach the track either take a van running along the Leeward Highway and ask to be put down at the junction with the Mount St Andrew road, or walk from Kingstown.

Large catamaran for cruises and speed boats for excursions as well as deep-sea fishing, snorkelling, dolphin and whale watching and land tours, cycling, birdwatching and jeep safaris. **HazECO Tours**, T784-4578634, www.hazecotours.com. Tours with emphasis on nature. Land tours, scenic tours (jeep safari tours) and boat tours. **Sam's Taxi Tours**, T784-4564338, www.samtaxiandtours.com. City tours (1-3 hrs), half-day tours (4 hrs) or full-day tours (6 hrs) including hiking the volcano. Yacht services and car rental.

Sea Breeze Nature Tours, T784-4584969, www.seabreezenaturetours.com. Hal Daize runs coastal boat tours of St Vincent as well as whale and dolphin watching, snorkelling and fishing charters.

⊖ Transport

St Vincent *p75, map p77*
Air
See page 76 for information on flights to the island. **Airport ET Joshua Airport**, small and rather chaotic, is 2 miles from Kingstown. The taxi fare to the Villa Beach area is EC$30 (with other fares ranging from EC$15-40 for nearer or more distant hotels set by government); minibus to Kingstown EC$1.50, 10 mins. Frequent and easy minibuses also run east if you need to get to Young Island or Calliaqua. The airport currency exchange desk is open Mon-Fri 0830-1230, 1530-1730, and is more convenient and quicker than a bank, Visa/MasterCard accepted.

Boat
See page 11 for how to get there by sea and box, opposite, for boat information.

Bus
Minibuses from Kingstown leave from the **Little Tokyo Fish Market** terminal to all parts of St Vincent island, including a frequent service to **Villa** and **Indian Bay**, the main hotel area; they stop on demand rather than at bus stops. At the terminal they crowd round the entrance competing for customers rather than park in the bays provided. They are a popular means of transport because they are inexpensive and give an opportunity to see local life. No service on Sun or holidays. Fares start at EC$1.50. **Sandy Bay** in the northeast is a difficult route because buses leave Sandy Bay early in the morning for Kingstown, and return in the afternoon. The number of vans starting in Kingstown and running to **Owia** or **Fancy** in the north is limited. The best way is to take the early bus to Georgetown and try to catch 1 of the 2 vans running between Georgetown and Fancy. To get to **Richmond** in the northwest take a bus to Barrouallie and seek transport from there.

Car hire
Avis, at the airport, T784-4566861, 0800-2100. There are several local companies; the tourist office has a list.

Cycling
Cycling is rewarding. The ride between Layou and Richmond is a strenuous 4 hrs one way, but absolutely spectacular. Expect long, steep hills and lots of them. Be careful in the north, which is a drug producing area. Contact **Sailor's Wilderness Tours**, Middle St, T784-4571712, http://sailorswildernesstours.com, owned by Trevor 'Sailor' Bailey, for escorted hiking and mountain biking, a subsidiary of **Sailor's Cycle Centre**.

Taxi
Taxis are not metered and fares are fixed by the Government, but you

Boat information

Ports of entry (own flag) Kingstown, Chateaubelair and Wallilabou on St Vincent, Port Elizabeth on Bequia, Britannia Bay on Mustique, Charlestown Bay on Canouan and Clifton Harbour on Union Island. All ports are operated by the **SVG Port Authority**, www.svgpa.com.

Anchorages Wallilabou, Young Island, Petit Byahaut, Blue Lagoon, Barefoot Yacht Charters Marina, Barrouallie, Buccament Bay Marina, Chateaubelair, Cumberland Bay, Kingstown Yacht Dock, Lagoon Marina, Ottley Hall Marina & Shipyard, Troumakar Bay, Bequia (Friendship Bay, Admiralty Bay, Moonhole, Bequia Marina, Daffodil Marina, Tony Gibbons Beach, Tradewinds Yacht Club), Palm (Prune) Island, Mustique (Britannia Bay), Canouan (Charlestown Bay, Tamarind Beach Hotel & Yacht Club), Isle à Quatre, Mayreau (Salt Whistle Bay, Saline Bay), Tobago Cays, Union Island (Anchorage Yacht Club, Bougainvilla Marina, Clifton, Frigate Island, Chatham Bay), Petit St Vincent.

Private yachts are required to pay a 'cruise tax' to Customs of EC$5 per person per day up to a maximum of EC$35, or seven days. If you leave SVG waters and then return you have to pay again. **Charter yachts** will pay the tax on your behalf. Vincentians, crew and children under 12 are exempt.

must check with the driver first to avoid overcharging. Late at night and early morning fares are raised. Tip about 10%. Kingstown to airport EC$25; Kingstown to Villa, Calliaqua EC$30; Kingstown to Layou EC$55. The **SVG Taxi Association**, Cruise Ship Berth, Kingstown, T784-4571807, svgtaxi@live.com, has a full list of drivers and fares, see also www. svghotels.com/member/svg-taxi-association. Taxi drivers are usually knowledgeable guides.

ⓘ **Directory**

St Vincent *p75, map p77*
Medical services Milton Cato Memorial Hospital, Kingstown, T784-4561185. **Pharmacy**: The People's Pharmacy, Greenville St, Kingstown, T784-4561170, Mon-Sat 0800-2000.

The Grenadines

The Grenadines, divided politically between St Vincent and Grenada, are a string of 100 tiny rocky islands and cays stretching across some 35 miles of sea between the two. They are still very much off the beaten track as far as mass tourism is concerned, but are popular with yachtsmen. The southern Grenadines are particularly beautiful, a cluster of picturesque, hilly islands with glorious white-sand beaches and rocky coves, excellent harbours and lots of opportunities for snorkelling, diving and other water sports. The Grenadines have a certain exclusivity, some of the smaller islands are privately owned and Mustique is known for its villas owned by the rich, royal and famous. There are some fabulously expensive and luxurious places to stay, but there are also more moderate hotels, guesthouses and rental homes for those who don't want to spend all their time afloat.

Arriving in the Grenadines

Getting there **Grenadine Air Alliance**, http://grenadine-air.com, a merger of **Mustique Airways**, **Trans Island Air** and **SVG Air**, operates daily shared charter services from Barbados to St Vincent, Mustique, Bequia, Union Island and Canouan and inter Grenadine scheduled flights from St Vincent to the same islands.

All the ferries are cheap and cheerful and an excellent way of getting around if the sea is not too rough. The *Barracuda* is the islands' 'mail boat' and carries everything, families and their goods, goats and generators; she rolls through the sea and the trip can be highly entertaining. There are several other ferries, more comfortable and faster, doing a variety of routes, see page 11. For other services, check at the Grenadines dock in Kingstown. There are often excursions from Kingstown to Bequia and Mustique on Sunday. Throughout the Grenadines power boats or yachts can be hired to take small groups of passengers almost any distance. Try to ensure that the boat is operated by someone known to you or your hotel to ensure reliability. Prices are flexible.

Getting around Bequia and Union Island have a limited system of public transport comprising minibuses and open-topped pick-up trucks (dollar bus), but the smaller islands do not. Taxis are the only other option, or walk.

Bequia → *For listings, see pages 113-124.*

Named the island of the clouds by the Caribs (pronounced Bek-*way*), this is the largest of the St Vincent dependencies. Nine miles south of St Vincent and about seven miles square, Bequia attracts quite a number of tourists, chiefly yachtsmen but also the smaller cruise ships and, increasingly, land-based tourists. The island is quite hilly and well forested with a great variety of fruit and nut trees.

Port Elizabeth and around

Its main village is Port Elizabeth and here Admiralty Bay offers a safe anchorage. Boat building and repair work are the main industry. Experienced sailors can sometimes get a job crewing on boats sailing on from here to Panama and other destinations. When you get off the ferry you will find to your left the fruit and veg market, with some clothes stalls and souvenirs.

Straight in front of you is the green-roofed **tourist information** ⓘ *T784-4583286, www.bequiatourism.com, Mon-Fri 0830-1800, Sat 0830-1400, Sun 0830-1200*, run by the **Bequia Tourism Association**. (They publish *Bequia This Week*, which has daily listings of what's on.) Across the road is the administration and finance building, and next to it is the Bayshore Mall, a blue and white building which contains a bank, a few shops and airline offices. The Anglican **St Mary's Church** was built of local limestone and ballast bricks in 1829, replacing an earlier church which was destroyed by a hurricane in 1798. It is open and airy and has some interesting memorial stones. The southern part of the bay is known as **Belmont**, where a waterfront walkway runs past hotels, restaurants, bars and dive shops on the narrow strip of sand.

Above and to the north of Port Elizabeth a paved road runs to **Hamilton Village** and the **Hamilton Battery**, which used to guard the bay. The original structure is no more, but French and British cannon retrieved from local waters have been placed there, looking out to sea. The view is indeed very fine over the harbour.

The west coast is the location for several yacht races, including the **Bequia Easter Regatta**. The centre of activities is the **Frangipani Hotel**, which fronts directly on to **Admiralty Bay**. There are races for all sizes and types of craft, even coconut boats chased by their swimming child owners or model sailing yachts chased by rowing boats. Everyone is welcome and there are crewing opportunities. There are other contests on shore (sandcastle building) and the nights are filled with events such as dancing, beauty shows and fashion shows.

Bequia

Where to stay 🛏
Bequia Beach **5**
De Reef Apartments **3**
Firefly Plantation Bequia **11**
Frangipani **4**

Gingerbread **6**
Julie & Isola's
  Guest House **7**
Keegan's Guesthouse **12**
KingsVille Apartments **8**

Old Fort Country Inn **9**
Ramblers Rest
  Guest House **1**

Cricket Grenadine style

Cricket is played throughout the Grenadines on any scrap of ground or on the beach. In Bequia, instead of the usual three stumps at the crease, there are four, and furthermore, bowlers are permitted to bend their elbows and hurl fearsome deliveries at the batsmen. This clearly favours the fielding side but batsmen are brought up to face this pace attack from an early age and cope with the bowling with complete nonchalance. Matches are held regularly, usually on Sundays, and sometimes internationals are staged. In Lower Bay v England, which Lower Bay usually wins, the visitors' team is recruited from cricket lovers staying in the area. It is best to bat at number 10 or 11.

To Mount Pleasant and Hope Bay

The walk up **Mount Pleasant** from Port Elizabeth is worthwhile (go by taxi if it is too hot), the shady road is overhung with fruit trees and the view of Admiralty Bay is ever more spectacular. There is a settlement of airy homes at the top, from where you can see most of the Grenadines. There is a general store with a restaurant and bar which sometimes has entertainment by local string bands in season. By following the road downhill and south of the viewpoint you can get to **Hope Bay**, an isolated and usually deserted sweep of white sand and one of the best beaches. At the last house (where you can arrange for a taxi to meet you afterwards), the road becomes a rough track, after half a mile turn off right down an ill-defined path through cedar trees to an open field, cross the fence on the left, go through a coconut grove and you reach the beach. The sea is usually gentle but sometimes there is powerful surf, a strong undertow and offshore current, so take care.

The west coast beaches

The nearest beach to Port Elizabeth is the pleasant **Princess Margaret beach** which shelves quickly into the clear sea. It was named after the princess in 1958 when she swam there while visiting the island by yacht. However, access is deliberately made difficult and there are no beach bars to spoil this stretch. Water taxi is the best way of getting here. At its south end there is a small headland, around which you can snorkel from **Lower Bay**, where swimming is excellent and the beach is one of the best on the island. Avoid the manchineel trees when it rains or you will get blisters. Local boys race their home-made, finely finished sailing yachts round the bay. In the village there are several places to stay as well as good restaurants and bars on the beach and up the hillside. Lower Bay gets very busy at holiday times.

The east coast

Away from the west side of the island the beaches are empty. Take a taxi over the hills to the east coast and the wild beaches on that side of the island. There are bigger trees on the Windward side, including hard woods such as white cedar, used for making boats.

Drive through coconut groves to **Spring Bay**, where there is a hotel and many desirable villas offering a tranquil outlook and breezy living. Spring Plantation once dominated this part of the island and the ruins of the old sugar mill can still be seen. **Firefly Plantation Inn** ① *T784-4583414, www.fireflyhotels.com, EC$10*, is built on the foundations of the old plantation house. Sugar is no longer grown but you can tour the 30-acre grounds with the head groundsman, who will show you the orchards of oranges, grapefruit, bananas, breadfruit, guava, Bequia plums, sour cherries, mangoes and other tropical produce and animals, let you sample the fruits and vegetables and tell you something about the estate's history.

Industry Bay has another nice beach, known as Crescent Beach, surrounded by palms with a brilliant view across to Bullet Island, Battowia and Balliceaux where the Black Caribs were held before being deported to Roatán. Food and drink available at the **Industry Beach Bar**. Both beaches are narrow with shallow bays and a lot of weed, making them less good for swimming and snorkelling. In the wet season there can also be a lot of runoff from the hills.

In the northeast corner of the island, at Park Beach, is **Old Hegg Turtle Sanctuary** ① *T784-4583245, oldhegg@vincysurf.com, EC$10/US$5 entrance fee, but donations warmly welcomed*, an extremely worthwhile conservation project to save the hawksbill turtle (*Eretmochelys imbricata*). Founded and maintained by a Bequian, a former fisherman, Orton 'Brother' King, local people contact him if they see turtles hatching and he goes to the beaches to collect them, releasing them into the wild when they are about 2½ years old. There is only about a 50% success rate and a lot of injuries from the turtles biting each other, but it is still better than the natural survival rate. A few green (*Chelonia mydas*) and leatherback (*Dermochelys coriacea*) turtles can also be seen in the tanks. Larger tanks are needed if the enterprise is to improve its success rate.

The south coast

Friendship Bay on the south coast is particularly pleasant, with a long sandy beach; there is some coral but also quite a lot of weed. It takes about 30 minutes to walk from Port Elizabeth to the **Friendship Bay Hotel**, at the east end of the bay, or a taxi costs EC$15. Alternatively, take a dollar bus (infrequent) in the direction of Paget Farm, get out at the junction (EC$1.50) and walk down to the village of La Pompe west end of the bay. There are a couple of hotels with restaurants and bars as well as rental villas and apartments and a dive shop.

Fishing boats are drawn up on the beach and building and sailing model boats is a favourite local pasttime.

At **Paget Farm**, whale harpooning is still practised from February to May (the breeding season) by a few fishermen who traditionally use three 26-ft long cedar boats, powered by oars and sails. However, power boats are now used sometimes and many of the traditions have been lost.

If you can arrange a trip to **Petit Nevis**, to the south, you can see the whaling station and find out more about Bequia's whaling tradition. Despite pleas from conservationists, a humpback mother and calf have several times been harpooned off Bequia. Bequia has an annual quota of four whales and with traditional technology and power it is easier to kill a calf and then its mother than an adult male. In 2012 the International Whaling Commission renewed St Vincent and the Grenadines' licence for the annual slaughter until 2018. Several whalers have given up the practice and it is hoped that the licence will not be renewed again. There is a whaling museum on the way to Paget Farm, **Athneal's petite museum** ① *US$2*, which has whale bones, old photos and tools of the trade.

The tourist office can help you visit the cliffside dwellings of **Moon Hole**, at the southwest, where a rocky arch frames the stone dwelling and the water comes up the front yard. It is a private, secluded development of some 20 homes and rental villas built in the rocks above a pristine white sand beach.

Mustique → *For listings, see pages 113-124. See map, page 106.*

Lying 18 miles south of St Vincent, Mustique is three miles long and less than two miles wide. In the 1960s, Mustique was acquired by a single proprietor who developed the island as his private resort where he could entertain the rich and famous. It is a beautiful island, with fertile valleys, steep hills and 12 miles of white sandy beach, but described by some as 'manicured'. The whole of the island, its beaches and surrounding waters are a conservation area. It is no longer owned by one person and is more accessible to tourists, although privacy and quiet is prized by those who can afford to live there. Most visitors are day-trippers from Bequia or other neighbouring islands on private or chartered yachts, who stay on the beach and eat at **Basil's**. There is no intention to commercialize the island and in fact the management company has a reputation of trying to discourage casual visitors; it has only one petrol pump for the few cars.

The main anchorage is **Britannia Bay**, where there are 18 very expensive moorings for medium-sized yachts with waste disposal and phones. Take a picnic lunch to **Macaroni Beach** on the Atlantic side. This white-sand beach is lined with small palm-thatched pavilions and a well-kept park/picnic area. Swimming and snorkelling is also good at **Lagoon Bay**, **Gallicaux Bay**, **Britannia Bay** and **Endeavour Bay**, all on the leeward side. **L'Ansecoy Bay** in the north is a wide beach, notable for the wreck of the French liner the *Antilles*, which went aground offshore in 1971.

Basil's Bar and Restaurant is *the* congregating spot for yachtsmen and the jet set. Snorkelling is good here too. From here there is a well beaten path to the **Cotton House Hotel**, which is the other congregating point.

Canouan → *For listings, see pages 113-124.*

A quiet, peaceful crescent-shaped island, Canouan lies 25 miles south of St Vincent, with excellent reef-protected beaches. Evidence of human occupation dates back to 200 BC, pendants and pottery shards having been found during construction work on the airport and hotels. The island was valuable for plantation crops during the colonial period, namely sugar then cotton, which was grown until 1924. The Snagg family who owned the land were unable to keep the plantation going and the north reverted to acacia scrub and thicket. The estate was sold to the government in 1946. Other local families include the Comptons and the Mitchells, shipwrights who arrived in the

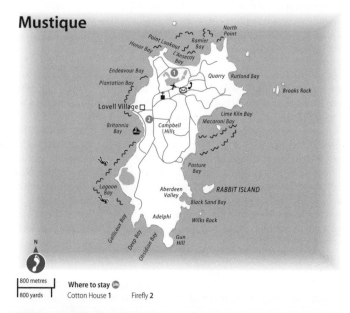

Mustique

Where to stay
Cotton House **1**   Firefly **2**

19th century. At that time there was plenty of cedar (for the hull), mahogany (for planking) and bamboo (for masts) for ship building. In 1939 Reginald Mitchell built the largest schooner ever in the Lesser Antilles. The three-masted *Gloria Colita* was 165 ft long, 39 ft wide and weighed 178 tons. Unfortunately only two years later it was found abandoned and awash in the Gulf of Mexico and no one knows what happened to Captain Mitchell and his crew.

The village, on the leeward side in Grand Bay, is **Charlestown**, founded after a devastating hurricane destroyed the settlement at Carenage Bay in 1921. It is architecturally uninteresting, untidy and scruffy, having grown too quickly and unplanned, but the white-sand beach is superb, running the length of the bay and broken only by the jetty. On holidays, day trips are organized from St Vincent and then the beach is full of people. Cricket matches are held on the sand, ranging from little boys to family groups to serious young men who carefully measure their wicket and dispute calls. Balls constantly go in the water and stumps are made of any sticks found on the beach. The beach in the southwest by the airport is also splendid with white sand and views of numerous islands to the south. **Mahault Bay** on the north coast is beautiful, isolated, with steep hills all around, and great for a picnic. Turtles come here to nest.

Canouan

| | 0 metres 500 | | |

Where to stay		
Anchor Inn 3	Canouan Resort 1
	Tamarind Beach 2

Much of the north of the island, 800 of the island's 1866 acres, is owned by the Canouan Resort Development Company (CRD) and is now taken up by the **Canouan Resort at Carenage Bay**, a villa development and the **Tamarind Beach Hotel**. Access is gated and only employees and guests are allowed entry; all visitors need permission. There are two nice beaches, but being on the windward side the sea is often choppy and has a fair amount of weed. The beaches are open to the public, up to the high water mark, but access has to be from the sea, making a visit problematic unless you are a hotel guest or have your own boat. The centre of the bay is taken up with a golf course running up and over the hill.

Dive trips can be arranged through **Canouan Scuba Centre** beside the **Tamarind Beach Hotel**. The hotels organize boat trips to the Tobago Cays and non-hotel guests are permitted to make up numbers if the boat is not fully booked. The **Grenadines Estate Golf Club** is an 18-hole, par 72 course designed by Jim Fazio at the **Canouan Resort**. It covers 60 acres along the bay and up the hillside, giving lovely views of the sea. Rental equipment and buggies are available.

Mayreau → *For listings, see pages 113-124.*

Mayreau is small privately owned island with deserted beaches, one (closed) hotel and one guesthouse. It is only 1½ square miles and 254 people live there, mostly descendants of slaves imported by the Saint-Hilaire family who acquired the island after fleeing France in the Napoleonic Wars. The Eustace family inherited it through marriage on the death of Miss Jane-Rose de Saint-Hilaire in 1919 and their descendants still own all but 22 acres purchased by a Canadian family and 21 acres belonging to the government of St Vincent, on which the village is built. The village, with no name, is tightly packed on the hillside above the harbour. You can reach it only by boat and the ferry calls on its way from St Vincent to Union. There is no deep water dock, though, so goods and passengers are offloaded into little boats and dinghies which then struggle to the jetty in great danger of being swamped by a wave. The beaches are glorious and Mayreau is a popular stop-off point for yachties, particularly in **Salt Whistle Bay**, a perfect horseshoe-shaped bay in the northwest, on a spit of land with a long, wild beach on the other side, which is to windward. Many day charters include the bay as a useful lunch stop when visiting the Tobago Cays.

Tobago Cays → *For listings, see pages 113-124.*

The Tobago Cays are a small collection of islets just off Mayreau, protected by a horseshoe reef and surrounded by beautifully clear water. The beaches are some of the most beautiful in the Caribbean and there is diving and snorkelling on **Horseshoe Reef** and wall. Turtles are commonly seen and there are lots of colourful fish. A turtle-watching area has been marked by buoys around the beach on Baradel cay. You should go no closer than six feet from a turtle, although it may approach you, in which case you should stay still.

Anchor damage, together with hurricanes, over-fishing and removal of black coral, killed some of the reef; hard coral lies broken on the bottom, but overall it is in remarkably good condition considering the volume of visitors it receives. After long negotiations, the government bought the Tobago Cays in 1999 and, as a result of the pressure on the ecology, **Tobago Cays Marine Park** ⓘ *T784-4858191, http://tobagocays.org*, was formed. It is a national park and wildlife preserve, which covers four uninhabited cays, the 4-km Horseshoe Reef and a 1400-acre sand-bottom lagoon. It has not always been well policed, but rangers will come to collect a fee of EC$10 per person per day. A six-knot speed limit is in force for all craft. Scuba diving may only be done with a registered local dive shop, not independently. Do not touch anything underwater, coral dies if you do. No fishing is allowed.

Mayreau & the Tobago Cays

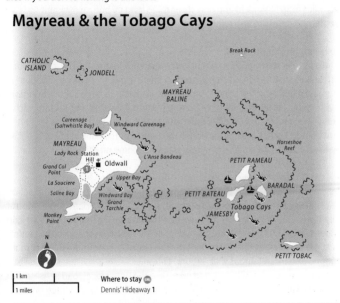

1 km
1 miles

Where to stay 🛏
Dennis' Hideaway 1

The Tobago Cays are crowded with unlimited charter boats, liveaboard boats or day charter catamarans out of St Vincent, Bequia, Canouan and Union Island which can number over 150 in high season. Mooring buoys have been put in to prevent anchoring on the reef, but there are not enough. Although the yachts anchor on sand, their dinghies do not and they damage the coral if they put down anchor wherever they want to snorkel. The flat, calm water within the reef has become popular as a place to kitesurf. Although exhilarating, it is extremely dangerous with so many swimmers and snorkellers on the surface of the water. There are also anchorages in the cut between Petit Rameau and Petit Bateau, or to the south of Baradel.

You can shop at your boat or on the beach: ice, butter, fresh fish, lambi, lobster, T-shirts, even French designer clothes are brought to you by boat men. Don't give them your garbage though, or you'll be sunbathing next to it on the beach later.

The Tobago Cays were used for the filming of *Pirates of the Caribbean*, and the *Scaramouche*, a two-master boat, used for taking tourists to the cays, was converted into an impressive Portuguese merchant ship.

Union Island → *For listings, see pages 113-124.*

The most southerly of the islands belonging to St Vincent, Union Island is 40 miles from St Vincent and only three miles long by one mile wide. It has two settlements, **Clifton** and **Ashton**.

Arriving on Union Island

Clifton serves as the south point of entry clearance for yachts. The immigration office and customs are at the airport, so if you arrive by boat you check in at the **Yacht Club** and the airport. Similarly on departure, check out at the airport, even if you are leaving by ferry from Ashton to Carriacou. For visiting yachts there are anchorages at Clifton, Frigate Island and Chatham Bay, while the **Anchorage Yacht Club** marina has some moorings. The **tourist office** ① *T784-4588350, daily 0900-1600*, is on your left as you come off the ferry.

Places on Union Island

Seventy-five per cent of the population live in Ashton, but 95% of the action takes place in Clifton. Union is distinguished by some dramatic peaks. **Mount Olympus** (637 ft) is in the northwest, while **Mount Parnassus** (920 ft) and **Mount Taboi** (1002 ft) stand side by side in the centre-west and in the centre-east are the jagged **Pinnacles** (925 ft). The landscape around Ashton is more rugged and mountainous than around Clifton.

Parnassus, or 'Big Hill', is a good hike. Take the upper level road in Ashton. In front of a clearing are some steps leading to a path. After two or three minutes, fork to the left. The path winds round the hill to the top, from where the views are as fine as you would imagine.

North of the airport is **Fort Hill** (450 ft), where the site of a 17th-century French fort gives a panoramic view of dozens of islands. A walk around the interior of the island (about two hours Clifton–Ashton–Richmond Bay–Clifton) is worth the effort, with fine views of the sea, half a dozen neighbouring islands, pelicans and Union itself.

The beach at **Chatham Bay** is beautiful and deserted, but not particularly good for swimming as there is a coral ledge along most of it just off the beach. Snorkelling and diving are good, though. It is one of the last undeveloped anchorages in the Grenadines. There is no road and you have to walk 30 minutes along a footpath through the bush from the end of the road just above Ashton down to the bay. Women should not go there alone, there have been reports of attacks.

Bloody Bay has a long, sandy beach, best reached from the sea, although there is some surf. **Richmond Bay** is also pleasant, good for swimming and easily reached as the road runs alongside it. However, it is dirty and there is broken glass on the sand, so take care. Round the point, **Belmont Bay**, or Big Sands, is another sandy beach, with a small hotel.

There is also a 20-berth marina at **Bougainvilla** ① *T784-4588678, www.grenadines-bougainvilla.com*, a smart complex of businesses next to the **Anchorage**, offering accommodation, a restaurant, a boutique, a wine shop, internet access and laundry at **Erika's Marine Services** (see below), the offices

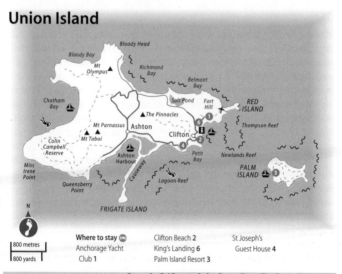

Union Island

Bloody Head
Bloody Bay
Mt Olympus ▲
Richmond Bay
Belmont Bay
Chatham Bay
Salt Pond
Fort Hill
RED ISLAND
▲ The Pinnacles
Mt Parnassus ▲ ▲
Ashton
Mt Taboi ▲
Clifton
Thompson Reef
Colin Campbell Reserve
Ashton Harbour
Petit Bay
Newlands Reef
Miss Irene Point
Causeway
Lagoon Reef
PALM ISLAND
Queensberry Point
FRIGATE ISLAND

N

800 metres
800 yards

Where to stay 😴
Anchorage Yacht Club **1**

Clifton Beach **2**
King's Landing **6**
Palm Island Resort **3**

St Joseph's Guest House **4**

of Moorings, VPM Dufour Yachting, Bamboo Yachting, Oversea Sailing, Star Voyage, Wind and Sea Ltd (cruise ship agent and charter), and Unitech Marine supply and repair.

A good reason to visit Union Island is to arrange day trips to other islands or to find a ride on a yacht to Venezuela towards the end of the season (May-June). Day trip boats to other islands leave from Clifton around 1000. Erika's Marine is a good place to find and book a suitable tour. Yannis Tours ① T784-4588513, arranges tours to the nearby Tobago Cays (see below), Palm Island, Petit St Vincent and other small islands. They have two large and comfortable catamarans, which are recommended if the sea is a bit rough, and provide breakfast, lunch, rum punch and soft drinks. Alternatively, you can spend a day on the *Scaramouche*, a traditional working schooner, used in the filming of *Pirates of the Caribbean*, the classic hand-built schooner, *Friendship Rose*, or hire a local skipper to take you in a smaller boat wherever you want to go. This is recommended if the sea is calm so that you can spend the maximum time snorkelling at the Tobago Cays. The SVG Water Taxi Association sets prices, so don't be fooled into a 'good rate'. Check at the tourist booth.

Petit St Vincent → *For listings, see pages 113-124.*

Locally referred to as PSV, this is a beautiful, privately owned, 113-acre island with one of the Caribbean's best resorts. At the Petit St Vincent you will find laid-back luxury, casual and stylish, with an excellent standard of service. If relaxation is what you want, you can get it here in spades. There are lots of trees and flowers providing a peaceful atmosphere and you can see most of the southern Grenadines from one view or another, even Mustique on a really clear day. The island is part of the Small Luxury Hotels of the World portfolio and has a staff to guest ratio of more than 2:1. Accommodation is in 22 secluded cottages mostly on the northeast side of the island, which have the most glorious views of the reef and the changing colours of the sea, encompassing all the blues and turquoises imaginable. Steps lead down the cliffs to the beach, where you can snorkel. There is a tree-top spa, tennis court, fitness track and water toys: sunfish, hobie cats, windsurfers, glass-bottom kayaks. You can have room service (especially nice for breakfast) or eat in the central building. Picnics can be arranged on the south-facing beach (hammocks and shade thoughtfully provided) or on the tiny islet Petit St Richardson. You can snorkel and dive off the Mopion and Punaise sandbar islands to the northwest. The island can be reached by charter flight from Barbados to Union Island and the resort's launch picks you up there. The anchorage and jetty are on the south side opposite Petite Martinique, protected by a reef. Beaches are public, so don't be surprised to see local children from Petite Martinique swimming or playing cricket near the anchorage.

Palm Island → *For listings, see pages 113-124.*

Also known as **Prune Island**, this is another privately owned, luxury resort, about a mile from Union Island, with coral reefs on three sides. The island was developed by John and Mary Caldwell, after they had made several ocean voyages. John was the author of *Desperate Voyage*, a book describing his first ocean crossing; with virtually no previous experience, he sailed from the USA to Australia to meet Mary. The boat was demasted, wrecked on a reef and John was stranded on an island and had to eat slime from his boat until he was rescued. The Caldwells later leased this low-lying swampy island from the St Vincent government and the family built the resort. Mary followed John in writing her own book about their early life together, *Mary's Voyage: The Adventures of John and Mary Caldwell – A Sequel to Desperate Voyage*.

There are four beaches, of which the one on the west coast, **Casuarina**, is the most beautiful, with the most sand. A casual bar and restaurant facing Union Island is open to yachties and passengers of small cruise ships, but the rest of the island is reserved for guests. Even access to the beach from the jetty is prevented by ropes and notices. Water purchase is possible for yachts, moorings available. Sailing, windsurfing, scuba diving, snorkelling, fishing, tennis and health club are all available, snorkelling and diving is usually on the Mopion and Punaise sandbar islands. Shared charter flights can be arranged from Barbados to Union Island, where you will be met and brought over by the resort's launch, 10 minutes.

⊙ The Grenadines listings

For hotel and restaurant price codes and other relevant information, see pages 13-16.

⊙ Where to stay

Bequia *p101, map p102*
Many villas are available for rent, see www.bequiatourism.com for a good selection of properties, or http://grenadine-escape.com.
$$$$ Bequia Beach, T784-4581600, www.bequiabeach.com. Lovely location and right on the beach, rooms, suites and villas, excellent service with owner and manager both around all the time. Very relaxing with 2 pools, reading room, spa, gym, water sports centre along the beach. Beachside or hillside restaurants, good food and drinks and entertainment some nights but there are lots of steps up to the Italian restaurant.
$$$$ Firefly Plantation Bequia, Spring Bay, T784-4888414, www.fireflybequia.com. Part of an 18th-century working plantation, set among coconut palms and fruit orchards on a hillside to catch the breeze. The height of luxury with service to match, very relaxing and lovely views. A good walk

to Port Elizabeth over the hills, or down to the turtle sanctuary.

$$$$ Gingerbread, Admiralty Bay, on Belmont walkway by the beach, T784-4583800, www.gingerbreadhotel.com. A very pretty small hotel with gingerbread fretwork. Suites with well-stocked kitchens overlooking Admiralty Bay in beautiful mature gardens steps from the walkway and access to restaurants. Good food, great café downstairs, with delicious ice cream and bakery, live music some nights, friendly host, Pat Mitchell.

$$$$ The Old Fort Country Inn, Mount Pleasant, T784-4583440, www.theoldfort.com. A boutique hotel or rental villa in a 17th-century French-built fortified farmhouse, probably oldest building on Bequia, magnificent views with a good breeze on top of the hill, quiet and peaceful, lovely pool with view of 25 islands, beach within walking distance or daily shuttle to other beaches.

$$$$-$$$ Frangipani, Admiralty Bay, T784-4583255, www.frangipanibequia.com. Cheaper rooms share cold water bathroom, garden units have private bathrooms and deluxe suites have fridge, good facilities and sea view, on beach or hillside along Belmont walkway, pleasant, mosquito net provided. The restaurant serves seafood and gourmet West Indian cuisine, snacks all day, don't miss the lime pie for dessert, jump-up and live music Thu, with steel band and barbecue buffet. The waterfront bar is a lovely place to while away the time with a cocktail.

$$$ De Reef Apartments, Lower Bay, T784-4583484. Good, well-equipped apartments of 1-2 bedrooms in gardens by the beach, a/c, fans, mosquito nets, terrace or balcony. Owner Joan is very helpful and accommodating. Lots of repeat visitors.

$$$ KingsVille Apartments, Lower Bay, T784-4583404, http://kingsvilleapartments.net. Run by Bert and Kay King, 1- or 2-bedroom apartments in cottages, right by the beach, a/c, modern, convenient for restaurants.

$$$-$$ Julie and Isola's Guesthouse, Port Elizabeth, T784-4583304. 2 locations, on Front St in block building overlooking the ferry dock with a/c, hot water and Wi-Fi, and Back St, 3 mins' walk away in old wooden building with fan, mosquito net and cold water, go to Front St for Wi-Fi. Attached restaurant, good local food, good cocktails in noisy bar downstairs, meeting place for travellers to form boat charter groups.

$$$-$$ Keegan's Guesthouse, Lower Bay, T784-4583530, www.keegansbequia.org. Lovely position on the beach, simple rooms, fan, mosquito nets, can include breakfast and evening meal, will cater for vegetarians, also 1- to 2-bedroom apartments, Wi-Fi, table tennis, volley ball, Sat night barbeque.

$$$-$$ Rambler's Rest Guesthouse, Port Elizabeth, T784-4300555, www.accommodation-bequia.com. Irishman Donnaka offers hiking tours, see below, and has converted his house into a small guesthouse with 2 rooms upstairs sharing a bathroom and a 2-bedroom apartment downstairs. 10-mins' walk uphill from village centre, Donnaka is friendly, informative and takes you around Port Elizabeth to show you where everything is.

Mustique *p105, map p106*

$$$$ Cotton House, T784-4564777, www.cottonhouse.net. Luxury hotel converted in 1968 by Oliver Messel from an 18th-century cotton warehouse into an elegant plantation house, very expensive, spa and fitness centre, pool, tennis, windsurfers, sailfish, snorkelling, all included, horse riding and scuba diving available, sailing packages tailor made.

$$$$ Firefly, T784-4563414, www.fireflymustique.com. On a hillside with lots of steps, small and intimate with house-party feel. All 5 rooms with view overlooking the bay, 2-tiered pool with a view, bar gets busy with celebrities and other home-owners in the evening.

$$$$ The Mustique Company Ltd, T784-4888000, www.mustique-island.com. 50 of the 82 private residences are available for rent, with staff, from US$5000 per week in summer for a 1-bedroomed villa to US$75,000 per week in winter for a large villa.

Canouan *p106, map p107*

$$$$ Canouan Resort at Carenage Bay & The Grenadines Estate Villas, T784-4588000, www.canouan.com. The largest and most luxurious resort in the Grenadines, with suites and villas, built to the highest specifications on a 1200-acre private estate. Several gourmet restaurants offering everything from caviar to pasta in pretentious surroundings.

Spa with treatment rooms dotted around the resort and even built out over the coral reef with glass floor. The fitness centre has private trainers, yoga and aerobics. Tennis centre with 4 all-weather, flood-lit courts and pro-shop, lots of water sports and water toys, day trips by boat. The golf course is one of the best in the Caribbean.

$$$$ Tamarind Beach Hotel and Yacht Club. Part of the Canouan Resort but less exclusive. Set in lovely mature gardens, green and lush, 45 comfortable rooms and suites, all with sea view and right on beach, everything wood and wicker, popular restaurant, humming with yachties at night, water sports, PADI dive shop on site. Grenadines base for **Moorings** yacht charter business, long dock for dinghies, moorings rather rolly, more comfortable sleeping to anchor in north corner of bay. They also provide water, ice, bread, showers, to yachties.

$$$ Anchor Inn, Grand Bay, T784-4588568. Close to the Tamarind, convenient location near the beach, apartments. There aren't many budget options on Canouan but this is worth trying.

Mayreau *p108, map p109*

$$$ Dennis' Hideaway, T784-4588594, www.dennis-hideaway.com. With the Saltwhistle closed, this is now the only place to stay: 5 twin or triple rooms with a/c, fans, fridge, balcony over looking the sea for a sunset view, bar, restaurant, good food and drinks at reasonable prices, pool with spectacular view, yacht charter, fishing trips, beach trips.

Union Island *p110, map p111*

$$$$ Anchorage Yacht Club, Clifton, T784-4588221, www.anchorage-union.com. Beside the runway, marina service, restaurant overlooking shark pool, terrace bar, rooms in cottages or an apartment for longer term rental, small beach. Kiteboarding centre, boat tours, fishing and diving, full moon beach parties.

$$$$-$$$ King's Landing, Clifton, T784-4588823, www.kingslanding hotel.com. Recently renovated, 17 rooms and bungalows in gardens on the harbour. Balcony, a/c, TV, Wi-Fi, fridge, large pool in the garden. Bungalows have kitchen and dining facilities. Breakfast included.

$$$ Clifton Beach Hotel and Guesthouse, T784-4588235, clifbeachhotel@caribsurf.com. The oldest hotel on the island, Adams family now in 3rd generation of innkeepers, open since 1952, now with a wide range of accommodation over 4 locations. Main guesthouse rooms on the waterfront, TV, kitchenettes, a/c available, fans, Wi-Fi. Old but comfortable, clean and friendly, meal plans available, restaurant overlooking water, laundry, friendly service, water and ice for boats, bike, car and jeep rental.

$$$ St Joseph's Guesthouse, Clifton, T784-4858335 at Erika's Marine Services, www.erikamarine.com. Guesthouse built just above the new RC church, stupendous views of Palm Island, Petit St Vincent, Petite Martinique and Carriacou, delightfully breezy and peaceful on the spacious balconies, pleasant apartments and

a cottage, all with kitchens, access to beach at the bottom of the hill, good snorkelling, jeep rental. You don't have to be religious to stay, all are made to feel at home.

Petit St Vincent *p112*

$$$$ Petit St Vincent Resort, PO Box 841338, Pembroke Pines, Florida 33084, T954-9637401, 800-6549326, www.petitstvincent.com. One of the Leading Small Hotels of the World. All meals, room service and all facilities. Activities include hobie cats, sunfish, windsurfers, glass-bottom kayaks, snorkelling, lit tennis court, speed boat and sailing boat for tours to Tobago Cays or elsewhere, massage and facials, yoga and meditation.

Palm Island *p113*

$$$$ Palm Island Resort, T44-(0)1245 459900, http://palmislandresortgrenadines.com. Very comfortable rooms, suites and beachfront bungalows. Lots of watersports and activities. For stays of less than 7 nights, the flight from Barbados is US$400, longer stays include the cost in the rate.

❼ Restaurants

Bequia *p101, map p102*
There is a wide range of restaurants, from gourmet French to local West Indian, with pizzas, burgers and sandwiches also on offer. Reservations are recommended in high season, particularly during the Easter Regatta, when things get very busy.

$$$ Coco's Place, T784-4583463, VHF 68. Lunch and dinner daily. Fabulous view over harbour, up on hill at end of bay, lovely balcony, friendly pub and local kitchen, good fish dinner, piano and live music.

$$$ De Reef, T784-4583958. Lovely position on the beach, popular with yachties and locals, informal bar and restaurant, curried conch or conch souse, fish, salads and sandwiches, 3-course meals, bar snacks, Sun lunch with music jam sessions in the afternoon, Sat seafood buffet dinner with live music. Service can be very slow. Check your bill.

$$$ Fernando's Hideaway, T784-4583758. Dinner only Mon-Sat. Local-style fresh food, short menu, fish caught by 'Nando, candlelit dinner, special goat water soup on Sat.

$$$ Fig Tree, Belmont Walkway, T784-4573008, www.figtreebequia.com. Wed-Mon Nov-Mar 0800-2200, Apr-Oct 1100-2000. Local meals, variety of rotis, fish, ribs, curried mutton, vegetarian options, reservations advised in high season for dinner. Fish fry on Fri very popular. Wi-Fi. Rooms available.

$$$ Mac's Pizzeria & Bakeshop, Belmont walkway, T784-4583474, beqvilla@caribsurf.com. Daily 1100-2200. Very popular, get there early or reserve in advance, also takeaways, 3 sizes, try the lobster pizza in season, pricey at EC$90 for a 9-inch one, but covered with lobster, don't add other ingredients. Extensive menu also includes sandwiches and snacks such as samosas and conch fritters and an assortment of freshly baked goods.

$$$ Tante Pearl's, T784-4573160, VHF 68. Open 1130-1400, 1730-late. West Indian cooking, lobster and conch, all the usual trimmings, up on Cemetery Hill 2 mins by taxi above Port Elizabeth up a very steep hill, nice breeze. Wonderful alcoholic or virgin cocktails, excellent sundowners with a great view.

$$$-$$ L'Auberge de Grenadines, Hamilton, north shore of Admiralty Bay (former Schooner's restaurant), T784-4573555, www.caribrestaurant. com. Lunch and dinner. Pretty setting with views over the water. French with emphasis on lobster in season, large tank of live specimens, lobster lunch, filling lobster burgers. Serve river lobster from St Vincent when out of lobster season. A la carte or 3-course set dinner. Live music, reservations advised.

$$$-$$ Porthole, at the start of the Belmont walkway, T784-4583458. Mon-Sat 0730-2100. Local Creole dishes, rotis for lunch, Mexican, fish, pickled conch, sandwiches. Noelina and Lennox Taylor run this low-key restaurant with a small grocery store at the back. Live music in season.

$$$-$$ Sugar Reef Café, Crescent Beach, T784-4583400, www.sugarreef bequia.com. Daily 1200-2100. Only local fish, meat, fruit and veg served here, using coconut instead of dairy with emphasis on healthy eating. Romantic setting on the beach with local wooden tables and driftwood chandeliers. Very busy in high season, when reservations are essential, but can be empty in low season. Also 8 rooms in the **Beach House** or **French House**, all on a 65-acre estate, a lovely place to stay.

$$$-$$ Whaleboner, Belmont walkway, T784-4583233. Mon-Sat 0800-2200, Sun 1400-2200. A fun place at the heart of local activity. Pleasant for breakfast or a cool beer at any time. Good barbeque. No credit cards. Friendly service, but check your bill.

Mustique *p105, map p106*
$$$ Basil's Bar, T784-4888350 for reservations, www.basilsbar.com. Kitchen open 0800-2200, bar open later. For seafood and nightlife, exclusive and expensive, Wed is good with barbecue and jump-up, Sun is sunset jazz and a cocktail.

On Sat go to the **Cotton House**. Reservations required at the **Cotton House** and **Firefly**.

Canouan *p106, map p107*
The hotel restaurants serve international food with local specialities. A few local restaurants have opened in the village and are much cheaper than the hotels. There is a bar by the ferry dock but it does not always serve food.
$$$-$$ Frontline, upstairs on the road opposite the road leading to the dock. Breakfast, lunch and dinner. Cinty and Aneka cook a great traditional breakfast of saltfish as well as local meals for lunch, although you can also get an inexpensive sandwich if you prefer. They bake their own bread. In the evening they cook fish or chicken and chips unless you request something different.
$$$-$$ Mangrove, 20 mins along the beach from the **Tamarind Beach Hotel** although it is easier to walk along the

road. Local place on the sand with tables indoors or under a manchioneel tree. The kitchen is made from a recycled shipping container. Good roti at lunch. Dinner options best chosen and reserved earlier in the day. Limited menu but lobster in season and steak. Watch out for rocks if you're arriving by dinghy. Live music Sat.
$$$-$$ Phyllis's Restaurant, on the main street by the junction with the road to the dock, T784-5934190. Lunch and dinner, but reservations advised in the evenings in case she doesn't open. Popular Thu barbecue from 1630 onwards.
$$$-$$ Thirsty Turtle, Glossy Bay, south coast, T784-4822224. Thu-Tue 1000-2300, lunch 1200-1345, dinner 1900-2045, pizza until 2145. On the beach, daily specials in the evening, mixture of local and Italian food with pizza and pasta as well as salads and sandwiches. Games and activities with themed nights.

Mayreau *p108, map p109*
$$$-$$ Combination Café, T784-4588561, VHF 16/68. Breakfast, lunch and dinner. Bar and restaurant with internet service. Dining on covered roof deck, good sunset views, West Indian and international dishes.
$$$-$$ Island Paradise, T784-4588941. Up the hill, everything fresh, good lobster, fish and curried conch, half price happy hour 1800-1900, barbecue Fri with local band, free ride up, skipper's meal free with more than 3 for dinner.
$$$-$$ J & C Bar and Restaurant, T784-4588558. Just beyond **Dennis'**

up the hill, best view of the harbour with soft music, boutique, room for a large group, good lobster, fish and lambi, for parties of 4 and over the captain's dinner is free.

Union Island *p110, map p111*
$$$ Barracuda, Clifton, T784-4588571, see facebook. Italian restaurant and bar with authentic pasta and pizza as well as some more local dishes. Good food and friendly service and atmosphere. Repainted and renovated in 2014.

$$$ Big Citi, Main St, Clifton, above the tourist office, T784-4588960. Mon-Sat 0800-2130 for food. Veranda seating with view over the street where the fruit and veg sellers are. Dependable grill, with meat and seafood options or sandwiches at lunchtime. Beer available but bring your own wine if you want it, no corkage charged.

$$$ Sparrow's Beach Club, Big Sand, T784-4588195, http://sparrowsbeach club.com. Come for the day and use the beach facilities (there's even a spa for massages), or for a romantic evening when the lights twinkle in the water. Bertrand runs this excellent French and Caribbean restaurant with flair, serving delicious food including his home-smoked marlin. The beer is cold and the wine list is good. A shuttle service to anywhere on the island makes it easy to get there.

☊ Bars and clubs

Bequia *p101, map p102*
Jump-ups and live music can be heard on different nights in the hotels and restaurants, including **Frangipani** and **Gingerbread**. Check bars for happy hours. There is something going on most nights either at Admiralty Bay, Lower Bay or Friendship Bay. Look in *Bequia This Week,* www.begos.com, which has daily listings. Bands play reggae music in the gardens of several hotels.

Mustique *p105, map p106*
Basil's Bar, see Restaurants. The centre of social life, Wed barbecue and jump-up, jazz most Sun nights, always lots of parties, music, DJ or house band to get you dancing, blues festival, see below. **Piccadilly**, up the hill from **Basil's**. The local pub, rotis and beer, and pool table; foreigners are welcome, but it is best to go in a group and girls should not go on their own.

Mayreau *p108, map p109*
Robert Righteous & de Youths Seafood Restaurant & Bar. Up a steep concrete road, you can't miss the colourful decor. Robert is a Rastafarian and the ramshackle place is decorated with flags, fishing paraphernalia and messages from yachties the world over. Food is available, but most people come for the drinks, the company, the music and the dancing. Robert, a well-known character, is always willing to partner anyone on the dance floor.

Union Island *p110, map p111*
Twilight Bar, near the main wharf in Clifton. Good drinks, the owner, Bert, sings and plays guitar most evenings.

O Shopping

Bequia *p101, map p102*
There are several marine stores and fishing tackle shops here.

Books
Bequia Bookshop, Port Elizabeth, T4583905. Run by Iain Gale, who keeps an excellent stock of books, particularly of Caribbean literature, maps and charts.

Crafts
Mauvin's and **Sargeant Brothers**' model boat shops (the latter up the hill going out of town), where craftsmen turn out replicas of traditional craft and visiting yachts. Many shops stock *Scrimshaw* knives, intricately designed and engraved by Sam McDowell, whose studio is at the **Banana Patch**, Paget Farm.
Noah's Arcade, at the **Frangipani** on Belmont walkway, T4583424. Mon-Fri 0900-1700, Sat-Sun 0900-1300. Is a branch of the enterprise on St Vincent, stocking gifts, books, handicrafts and the artwork of resident artists, whatever their origin.

Food
Bequia is a centre for yacht provisioning. There is a market for fruit and veg by the jetty and there are small supermarkets in Port Elizabeth with good selection of groceries and beverages but at higher prices than in St Vincent; fish is sometimes on sale in the centre by the jetty.

Canouan *p106, map p107*
Food
Canouan Food Ltd is on the main street in Charlestown, Mon-Sat 0800-2000, Sun 0900-1200, 1600-2000. Good selection and will deliver to the dock if you are on a yacht. There are also market stalls along the road from the dock.

Union Island *p110, map p111*
Food
Fruit and veg stalls line the road by the ferry dock, with the best of what's in season. There are a few supermarkets in Clifton which will deliver to the dock, and smaller groceries sell fresh produce and hardware.

O What to do

Bequia *p101, map p102*
Diving
Diving is good around Pigeon Island, afternoon and night dives are usually on the Leeward side of the southwest peninsula, there are a few sites around Isle à Quatre and shallow dives for training can be done around Petit Nevis.
Bequia Dive Adventures, Belmont walkway, next to **Mac's Pizzeria**, T784-4583826, VHF68 and 16, www.bequiadiveadventures.com. Full-service PADI dive centre. Diving and accommodation packages from US$700pp a week including 10 dives.
Dive Bequia, at the Gingerbread, Belmont, T784-4583504, VHF16 or 68, www.divebequia.com. Run by Bob

Sailing in the Grenadines

Sailing is excellent, indeed it was yachtsmen who first popularized the Grenadines and it is one of the best ways to see the islands. You can take day charter boats, easily arranged through hotels, or charter your own boat. There is a variety of boats for skippered day charters. Talk to the operators about size and predicted wind conditions if you are inclined towards seasickness. The large catamarans are usually quite stable so that you will hardly know you are on a boat, but they take quite large groups. If you hire a local yacht or motor boat for a day, make sure that the captain has life jackets and other safety equipment (eg a radio) on board and that he is properly insured. This may seem obvious, but do not take anything for granted and be prepared to ask lots of questions. A tourist and his son taking a short hop boat ride between islands found themselves drifting hopelessly off course when the boat's engine failed. The captain had no radio and they were eventually found several days later at death's door off the Venezuelan coast.

and Cathy Sachs. In operation since 1984, this company has the biggest boats, with shade and more room to move around and manoeuvre tanks and gear. US$130 for 2-tank dive including all gear, US$575 for PADI Open Water certification course.

Hiking

Brent Gooding T784-4952524, is an experienced guide who goes by the nickname of 'Bushman'. Flexible, tailor-made tours according to ability. Children under 12 free, 12-18 half price. **Ramblers Hiking Tours,** T784-4300555, www.hiking-bequia.com. Irishman Donnaka guides all abilities and tailors his tours to your interests, starting at 0800 in Port Elizabeth and ending somewhere where you can buy lunch or picnic on a beach, EC$120 per person.

Sailing

Friendship Rose is an 80-ft auxiliary schooner, T784-4583373, www.friendshiprose.com. US$150pp for day-long cruise 0700 or 0800-1730 to Tobago Cays, US$140 to Mustique, all-inclusive with meals, hammocks on board, deck cushions, snorkelling gear, launch for island exploring.
Octopus, T784-4325201, www.octopus-caribbean.com. Day sails or overnight cruises to Mustique, the Tobago Cays, Isle-à-Quatre on a 63-ft yacht accommodating 8 people for day sails and 2-6 for overnight charters.
Quest is a 44-ft centre cockpit yacht sleeping 2-7 people, based at Paget, T784-4583917, www.vrbo.com/453887. Skippered by Johnny Ollivierre, who also has **Petrel**, a 47-ft Swan for day trips to Mustique.

Tennis

Tennis can be played at the **Gingerbread** and **Frangipani** hotels.

Tour operators

Most tours of Bequia are little more than taxi tours taking around 3 hrs. Ask in the tourist office for the latest rates, or see a listing at www.bequia. net/carsjeepstaxis.html.

Union Island *p110, map p111*
Diving

Grenadines Dive, T4588138, www. grenadinesdive.com. Run by the very experienced Glenroy Adams, diving, mostly around the Tobago Cays.

Sailing

At Clifton, **Captain Yannis** has catamaran day tours starting in Union Island (early morning flights from other islands), visiting the Tobago Cays, Palm Island, etc, T784-4588513. Glenroy Adams of **Grenadines Dive** arranges customs clearance for yachtsmen in the southern Grenadines. **Sail Grenadines**, The Anchorage, Clifton, T784-5332909, www.sail grenadines.com. Offer day sails or longer cruises between the islands and starting from any of the islands.

⊖ Transport

Bequia *p101, map p102*
Air

JF Mitchell Airport has been built on reclaimed land with a 3200-ft runway, a terminal and night landing facilities, at the island's southwest tip.

Boat

Admiralty Transport Co Ltd, Brick House, Back St, Port Elizabeth, T784-4583348, http://admiralty transport.com and **Bequia Express**, T784-4583472, www.bequiaexpress. com, run ferries from **Kingstown** to Bequia (1 hr, EC$25 one way, EC$45 return with the same company). They start in Bequia, with the first one at 0630 Mon-Sat, 0700 on Sun; departing Kingstown at 0800. There are fewer crossings on Sat and fewer still on Sun and holidays.

Water taxis scoot about in Admiralty Bay, Princess Margaret Beach and Lower Bay for the benefit of the many yachts and people on the beach, whistle or wave to attract their attention, fare EC$15 per trip. For those arriving on yachts, there are **anchorages** all round either side of the channel in Admiralty Bay, Princess Margaret Beach, Lower Bay, Friendship Bay and off Petit Nevis by the old whaling station. Bequia Slipway has dockage, some moorings are available.

Bus

Buses (minivans and open pick-up trucks called dollar vans) leave from the jetty at Port Elizabeth and will stop anywhere to pick you up but do not cover the whole island; a cheap and reliable service.

Car

Car hire is available, cheaper if you rent for a week, try **Phil's Car Rental**, T784-4583304; **Handy Andy Rentals**, T784-4583722; Challenger Rentals, T784-4583811; or **Bequia Jeep**

Rentals, T784-4583760. If staying in an apartment, your landlord may already have an agreement with a supplier and can offer you a good deal.

Taxi

Taxis on Bequia, when not operating as buses, are pick-up trucks with benches in the back, brightly coloured with names like 'Messenjah'.

Mustique *p105, map p106*
Air

International connections are best through Barbados, a 50-min flight with **Mustique Airways**, www. mustique.com, although other connections are possible via Grenada and the neighbouring islands of **St Vincent**, **Bequia**, **Canouan** and **Union** with **SVG Air**, www.svgair.com. The airstrip, being in the centre of the island is clearly visible, so check-in time is 5 mins before take off (that is after you've seen your plane land).

Boat

The **Mustique Ferry**, T784-4571531, departs Mustique 0730 4 days a week for **St Vincent**, 2 hrs, returning 1400, US$10. *MV Barracuda, MV Gemstar* and *MV Canouan Bay* also call at Mustique on their way from Kingstown through the Grenadines, see page 11. Many people arrive on private or chartered yachts.

Canouan *p106, map p107*
Air

There is a good runway which has been extended on reclaimed land to take larger jets and a terminal building. There is a good service from Barbados (55 mins) or Grenada (20 mins) with **Grenadine Air Alliance/SVG Air** and **LIAT** (www. liat.com). These small planes also link Canouan with other islands nearby, **Martinique** (1 hr), **St Lucia** (40 mins), **St Vincent** (15 mins).

Boat

The main anchorage for yachts is **Grand Bay**. Others are at **Canouan Beach Hotel** and **Rameau Bay**, **South Glossy** and **Friendship** bays in settled weather. The *Barracuda* calls here on its way from St Vincent to Union Island and back twice a week, with occasional day trips at holiday times. See also page 11.

Union Island *p110, map p111*
Air

There are 5 main gateways for air services: St Lucia, Grenada, Barbados, St Vincent and Martinique, while there are also 5-min flights from Canouan and Carriacou. **Grenadine Air Alliance**, http://grenadine-air.com has daily flights from St Vincent. **SVG Air** and **Mustique Airways** offer charters.

Boat

There is an international ferry service between Ashton and Hillsborough on **Carriacou**, see page 12. The captain takes you through immigration procedures, but you should check out at Immigration at Clifton Airport the night before. Expect to have your bags thoroughly searched on arrival at Customs and Immigration at Hillsborough. If coming from

Carriacou to Union Island, get on the bus at Ashton and go to the airport for Immigration formalities. For ferry services with other islands in the St Vincent Grenadines, see page 11. The **SVG Water Taxi Association** sets rates for water taxis. From a yacht in harbour to land is US$2 per person during the day and US$3 per person at night. Clifton to **Ashton** or **Palm Island** is US$30 for 3-4 people one way, Chatham Bay, **Mayreau**, **Petit St Vincent** or **Petite Martinique** US$60.

Bus/bike/taxi

Minibuses run between Clifton and Ashton, EC$3. They convert to a **taxi** on request. **Bicycles** can be hired from **Erika's Marine Services**, T784-4858335.

ⓘ Directory

Bequia *p101, map p102*
Customs and immigration
On the main road by the dock, Mon-Fri 0830-1200 1300-1800, Sat 0830-1200 1500-1800, Sun 0900-1200, 1500-1800. Overtime fee may be charged outside office hours and on holidays. **Medical services** Bequia Casualty Hospital, Port Elizabeth, T784-4573328. **Police** Turn up the road by the banks, past the hospital and the police station is on your right before you get to the Clive Tannis Playing Field, T784-4583350, VHF16.

Canouan *p106, map p107*
Medical services Canouan Clinic.

Union Island *p110, map p111*
Customs Airport, T784-4588360, Mon-Fri 0830-1800. **Medical services** Hospital, T784-4588339; Harvey's Pharmacy, T784-4588596.

Contents

Footnotes

Index

Join us online...

Follow **@FootprintBooks** on Twitter, like **Footprint Books** on **Facebook** and talk travel with us! Ask us questions, speak to our authors, swap stories and be kept up-to-date with travel news, exclusive discounts and fantastic competitions.

Upload your travel pics to our **Flickr** site and inspire others on where to go next.

And don't forget to visit us at footprinttravelguides.com